dn. 6-

DREAMS: DISCOVERING YOUR INNER TEACHER

YOUR INNER TEACHER

Clyde H. Reid

1817

Harper & Row, Publishers, San Francisco

New York, Grand Rapids, Philadelphia, St. Louis
London, Singapore, Sydney, Tokyo, Toronto

Cover design: Tom Egerman

Cover art: "Castle of the Pyrenees" by Magritte,
© by ADAGP, Paris, 1958.

Scripture texts used in this work are taken from the *King James Version* of the Bible.

Copyright © 1983 by Clyde H. Reid.

Library of Congress Catalog Card Number: 82-51158

ISBN: 0-86683-703-5

Printed in the United States of America.

5

To my friends at Mountain View Community Church,
who have challenged, stimulated, loved,
and accepted me

CONTENTS

CONTENTS

ACKNOWLEDGMENTS

The writing of this book began in the Calgary, Alberta, apartment of a friend, Dr. Ronald Dougan. I owe him my thanks for his generous offer of a hideaway, complete with typewriter, stereo music, and a refrigerator.

I received encouragement from many friends, including Dr. Edith Wallace, who wrote the foreword; Merika Graham, who read the manuscript in its early form and made some very helpful comments; and Laura Dodson, who also read the manuscript and made excellent observations.

My gratitude extends to the friends in Mountain View Community Church who welcomed my visits to their dream-sharing groups. The clients and friends who have shared their dreams with me through the years also hold a place of gratitude and respect in my heart. The minister of Mountain View, Dr. John Lee, has been a good friend and support in my work of leading people to self-discovery.

Joann Hildebrand deserves my appreciation for her fine work on the manuscript.

FOREWORD

This book fills a significant gap in the dream literature. It is not a learned tome, meant for the professional, nor is it a popular do-it-yourself manual with simplistic explanations. It is—and is meant to be—helpful to the individual who seriously wants to find a connection to the world of dreams. It is for the person who wants to understand this rich inner world and find guidance for living.

Clyde Reid is well equipped for such an undertaking. A clergyman with a prolific writing career, he eventually dedicated his life to helping others with their deeper psychological problems. In preparation for this task, he has studied Jung's psychology deeply, applying it both on the inner and outer levels. In the course of this study, Reid spent some time at the original C. G. Jung Institute in Zurich, Switzerland.

The founder of the Center for New Beginnings can not stay put, nor fail to be alert to *new* ways of therapy. He seems to be particularly well equipped to lead people to their deeper sources, partly by means of the knowledge gained through dedicated search. In other words, he leads individuals to experiences that are already familiar to him. By using dreams and active imagination, he leads his clients with a gentle, sympathetic hand toward the kind of transformation that means true healing.

Dr. Reid is trying to give leads to the understanding of dreams to persons who, for one reason or another, are not seeking or finding a professional helper. He does, however, recommend seeking a professional counselor when the need seems great.

Clyde Reid aids the reader by opening up his own dreams and insights. He reveals shadow aspects as well as a luminous spirit with great frankness, hoping to encourage others to start on the difficult and often painful road to self-discovery.

Without stereotyping or oversimplifying, he systematizes an approach to dreams (see the dream-journal form on p. 104) for easy reference.

While giving the dreamer every opportunity to enhance contact with the inner self, Reid is also active with his clients when necessary. His idea of dreams as *invitations* is an original contribution. There are many dreams which Jung himself would follow, react to, but not analyze. The active picking up of the dream's "invitation" is the author's own uniquely personal method.

Jung was the first to stress that method alone is useless unless it suits the person who uses it. That is clearly demonstrated in this book. Not only does the "method" suit the author, but he makes it clear that it must respect the nature and individuality of the dreamer.

I am impressed by the way the author emphasizes the importance of the dreamer's relationship with his or her own "inner authority," the inner self. Reid teaches the use of active imagination to achieve this inner relationship. He says, "I believe that my experience and comfort with active imagination is contagious." Some people need to be guided and taught to take the reality of the psyche seriously so that they can then turn confidently to their own inner resources. This book serves as such a guide.

Reid is echoing an important perception of our time when he says, "This book is written with [the conviction that] it is now the time of the inner teacher."

I found this book stimulating. Even for the experienced person, it presents new insights and should be useful for the beginner as well.

I wish it the success it deserves.

Edith Wallace, M.D., Ph.D.
New York City
July 1982

PREFACE

I had just finished giving a speech on dreams. Geneice Johnson approached me, introduced herself as a representative of Winston Press, and suggested that I allow them to publish my approach to dreams as a book. I told her I would think about it.

Two weeks later, at 11 P.M., I put down what I was reading and stood up to go to bed. Instead, however, I found myself reaching for a pad of paper and a pen; I quickly sketched the outline for *Dreams: Discovering Your Inner Teacher*. That night I dreamed constantly of writing about dreams and working with people's dreams. I awoke knowing I was to write the book.

There are already excellent books on dreams. What unique contribution could a new book offer? The answer soon became clear: I would write a book, not for the experts who have been steeped in dream theory or in Jung's psychology, but for the average reader who wants help in examining and understanding dreams. *Dreams: Discovering Your Inner Teacher* is that book.

This book goes beyond most books on dreams in one important respect. It turns the dreamer back to his or her own inner resources to discover the meaning of the dream. The time has come for us to learn how to converse with and trust our own inner teacher.

There is a place for dream experts—those whom we can consult for their wisdom, experience, and knowledge. I have consulted such experts for years, and I would recommend that others do likewise when appropriate. But we must begin to trust our interior, archetypal wisdom more completely. The dream interpretations that come from within us are the ones that are most meaningful, because they are totally of our own soul's fabric. Thus my aim in this book is to speak of the inner teacher and to reveal methods for getting in touch with that powerful resource.

1

THE POWER OF DREAMS

I am paralyzed as two snakes coil around my neck.
They are poised, ready to strike. I am helpless, unable
to move a muscle. I want to call out for help, but I
know that any move will mean death. I remain motion-
less, terrified.

This was the dream of a young man. How should he understand it? What do the snakes represent? Is there any reality
to the danger they seem to portray? Dreams like this raise
many such questions. They may occupy our attention and
concern for days or even weeks. They sometimes awaken us
in the night with terror. They shake us and shape us, guide
and inspire us. Dreams can be very powerful and even
lifechanging. Dreams have meaning, and it is possible to
learn the language of your dreams so you can claim those
meanings for your conscious self. In *Dreams: Discovering*
Your Inner Teacher, I will offer some step-by-step methods
for working with your own dreams to discover some of those
meanings.

Dreams become more crucially important as we approach
a new era of human consciousness. There are many kinds of
dreams—sleeping dreams, waking dreams, visions, sudden
insights—all breakthroughs from the deeper, inner well of
human racial wisdom and from the inner self. We will need
them all as we attempt to pull ourselves up from the morass
of human ignorance, power madness, and ego-entrapment.

Ancient Greek philosophers like Democritus of Abdera
urged us to believe, "The mind is divine and the body is
evil." We interpreted this to mean that we should reject the

body, the intuitive function of the mind, and our unconscious dream selves, while embracing reason. It is now time to reclaim our bodies, our sexuality, our intuitive wisdom, and all those things we put on the shelf while overdeveloping the reasoning part of us. Dreams are an important vehicle for this crucial reclamation.

In my own experience, one dream from my early youth stands out. At the age of twenty, I had graduated from college and accepted an appointment as assistant dean of students at Bradley University. I thought my career was launched. I wanted to be in college administration, and to my delight I had that opportunity. But then I had the dream, a dream that changed everything.

I dreamed that Jesus appeared alongside me and said, "Are you ready to come and help me?" I replied, "Yes, I think I am."

I had never paid attention to dreams before that. I had no idea that dreams were important, nor that professional psychologists used dreams to treat their patients. But I knew this dream had grabbed me and would not let me go. I kept asking people whom I respected what they thought it meant. And then I didn't want to hear their answers. I was on my way as a college administrator, and I didn't want any interference. So I began my new job, and I loved it. It was everything I had hoped for. But I kept wondering about that dream. Finally, about nine months later, I resigned my new position and went off to study theology to see if there was anything in it.

The dream did not change my life, but my *response* to the dream did. The dream alone may not change us significantly, but the way we respond to the leading of the dream can. I have never regretted my change of career. I know it was what I was intended to do with my life, and had I ignored it, my energies and direction would have gone sour.

Today, people come to me regularly to work on their dreams. Quite often someone will come into my office and say, "Wow, I had a bad dream last night!" One rule of thumb in my work with dreams is that there is no such thing as a "bad" dream. There are dreams that scare us, shake us, wake us up in a panic. But is that bad? I usually feel encouraged when I hear people say their dream had enough energy in it to jar them out of their complacency, to wake them up to an issue they need to look at.

When the dream disturbs us, it means that something inside us, some part of our deep, unconscious self, is trying to get our attention. Those unconscious aspects may use very dramatic methods to jar us awake, to pay attention to them. We may dream there are dark, hooded figures pursuing us, an airplane exploding in a ball of flame near us, someone murdering another person. This is our unconscious rattling our cage, shaking us out of our lethargy, demanding that we pay attention to our inner self. I don't consider that bad.

I have known people to ignore the callings of the inner self and go on with their lives as though they had heard nothing. People will come for counseling with a "scary" dream and will admit that their work or their marriage has lost its meaning, has become dead and deadening to their spirit. Yet they will not give it up. They are afraid to sacrifice the security of something known for something unknown; they are afraid to risk. In spite of the leadings of their dreams, they continue with their deadening and deadly work. What they ignore is the fact that they should be just as frightened of going dead as of risking. At least risk contains possibilities, while continuing in a dead way has few. And what is the security we win by staying in a dead job? What do we have when it's all over? What do we gain if we keep getting a safe paycheck but lose our soul in the process?

I am saying that dreams can guide us in our outer lives. Dreams can show us we need to make a change. Dreams can point us in the direction we should take in our careers to fulfill our inner calling. Dreams can warn us we are headed for a disastrous marriage.

One basic assumption behind all this is that dreams are trustworthy. If we do not really believe that, we are not likely to make important life decisions based on those dreams. I will return to this discussion of basic assumptions in the next chapter. But I do trust my dreams deeply. I have found their guidance has continually helped me to open up to new adventure and growth. I don't always trust my interpretation of the dreams, but I do trust that dreams are trustworthy.

Dreams can also guide us in our inner lives. We do live on many planes at once. To speak of inner and outer is just one simplistic way of looking at those many levels. We lead an outer life in our work, our relationships, the way we order our lives. At the same time, we have an inner life of fantasy, anxiety, worry, wonderings, and mental wanderings. We often live by inner decisions made years ago. Our dreams can help us be more in touch with that deep, inner life that exists side by side with our outer life.

Our dreams can show us who we are. In fact, they can sometimes show us ourselves unmercifully. If we really want to know ourselves in the deepest ways, we need to record and study our dreams carefully. When I began to work on my dreams with a Jungian analyst in Zurich, Switzerland, I had already devoted much time to a variety of approaches to personal growth. The path of dream interpretation took me into yet further and deeper reaches of my nature I had not even suspected were there.

I remember an unsavory dream that showed me a part of myself I had not previously known. I dreamed that I was living in a rooming house. One of the roomers was a priest. Though a priest, he did not seem to belong to any particular denomination or religious group. He wore heavy wool suits and did not bathe very often. He smelled terrible. In fact, he smelled so bad that we asked him to sleep in his car!

The analyst with whom I was working at that time did her job correctly: She asked me, "And what part of you is that smelly priest?" I cringed. I protested that it was an unfair question. I squirmed in my chair. But within a minute I knew the answer. There is a self-righteous part of me that gets "preachy" sometimes, looking down on others who aren't perfect and forgetting that I'm not perfect either. I may be driving thirty-five in a thirty-miles-per-hour zone, and I will find myself condemning the "lawbreakers" who pass me driving forty miles per hour, when they are merely doing it better than I am. That hypocrisy, of which I am sometimes capable, really smells bad!

That dream showed me who I am. It showed me a part of my shadow self that I need to know so I can keep an eye on it. When I told my wife the dream and my new understanding, she replied, "Oh yes, I know that part." It was no surprise to her, nor probably to a lot of other people who know me. But it was a surprise to me, and it meant I had to look more deeply at that part of my nature.

There is a basic, very important life principle involved here. When confronted with the "smelly priest" part of myself, I had to make a choice. I could elect to ignore or deny the "smelly priest" and live as though I knew nothing about it. Or I could own it, claim it as a part of myself, and incorporate it into my self-image. This is extremely difficult for some people to do. They protect and defend an image of themselves that must not include anything negative or uncomplimentary. Such persons can not really learn any-thing from their dreams, because they are dedicated to that shiny self-image. I am not criticizing such persons; I know I did the same thing for many years.

For many people, such a shiny self-image is a matter of survival, a matter of life and death for their personality. They may have learned when very small that they were not acceptable if they did not do things in a particular way and earn the approval of their parents. So they are still busy winning that approval from everyone. For them, looking at the shadow side of their lives is very difficult. Yet when we learn to own those dark aspects, claim and admit that they are part of us, it is actually a great relief. We no longer need to hold up the heavy shield that deflects all criticism. We can join the human race that is imperfect just as we are. And the "smelly" parts of us become less dangerous because they are out in the open where we can keep an eye on them. But when we deny them and keep them pushed down in the basement, they can really hurt us because they sneak out when we are least aware.

Dreams can guide us in our personal growth. Many thousands of persons these days are turning to psychological leaders for help in understanding themselves. In contrast to turning to psychotherapy because of a crisis or disaster in their personal lives, they are turning to dream therapy and growth experiences to push back the boundaries of their personalities and help them know themselves more deeply. Dreamwork is one of the paths that is most useful in this personal growth endeavor.

Persons who really want to know themselves, shadows and all, are on a spiritual journey. For it is in the depths of the personality that we encounter the rich spiritual realities of the soul. For that reason, today there is a growing awareness of the common ground shared by psychology and spirituality. Indeed, a new branch of psychology, transpersonal psychology, is based on this fundamental truth. So the pursuit of our dreams may be understood as a spiritual pilgrimage—into the depths of the soul.

Dreams can guide us in mysterious ways. In early 1974, I was working with a group of friends to set up a nonprofit educational center where I could do my work with people and gather professionals who would share my convictions about the importance of personal growth. One friend had loaned us $20,000 and made an outright gift of another $5,000. The Lilly Endowment had made us a grant of $35,000 to get the project off the ground. We had found a building that seemed just right for our purposes. We had almost enough in loans to make the large down payment on the building and complete its purchase. But the bank was still hesitating on the final approval of the loan, unsure about our ability to meet mortgage payments.

It was in that climate of uncertainty that I had an interesting dream. I dreamed that two friends, Helen and Frank, were sitting together in their home. I walk up to Frank and ask him if I can borrow the keys to his airplane, as I have an errand in another city. (Frank really did have an airplane, and I had flown with him on several occasions.) He handed me the keys to the plane, and I went off on my errand.

A few days after the dream, I was at home on a Sunday afternoon. We were to have a final meeting with the bank within a few days to learn the fate of our application for the loan. My phone rang. Helen and Frank were on the phone, calling from their home in Montana. They told me they wanted to help start the new center but couldn't give a large amount of money. Instead, they were going to pledge to send $50 a month for the first year to help us get started. I was overwhelmed with their caring and generosity and told them so. It was a wonderful gift. I hung up and suddenly realized that they had just handed me the answer to our problems in acquiring the loan. I began phoning and writing other friends, asking if they would be willing to pledge a small amount each month for a year. When we walked into the bank later that week, we could show them pledges of $340 a month. The mortgage payments were to be $350 a month. One more $10 monthly pledge came in later, and for our first year of existence, the mortgage payments were assured! The bank promptly granted us the loan, the Center for New Beginnings was born, and since that day in 1974, thousands of persons have received personal help, growth, and education through that center. The dream provided the final key to unlock the vaults of the bank and make it all possible.

I repeat that dreams have great power. They can guide us in our decisions and force us to look at ourselves honestly. They can lead us deeper into the soul, change our whole life.

2

BASIC ASSUMPTIONS IN DREAMWORK

One of the most important assumptions in this book and in my work with people has to do with the nature of that part of our being we call the unconscious. Clearly, our everyday activities are deeply influenced by a part of us that is not directly available to our consciousness. The work of Sigmund Freud helped establish that fact forever. However, Freud made one fundamental mistake.

According to Freud, the unconscious contains only those memories and experiences which have happened to us since birth. The unconscious is like a bank vault, he said, storing memories until we may reopen the vault at some later time. The purpose of a Freudian analysis, then, is to empty the vault, recognize all the primitive and infantile memories and experiences locked in there, and clean it out. Then, presumably, you are whole.

It took Carl Jung, Freud's handpicked successor until they disagreed, to discover that the unconscious was much deeper, richer, and more mysterious than Freud had been willing to accept. For Jung, the unconscious was more like a deep well, reaching down into the earth and then opening into an underground ocean filled with psychic realities he called archetypes. The archetypes are basic motifs and psychic patterns that live in our deep unconscious and influence our lives constantly. The hero is one such archetype. It lives in all of us, causes us to be drawn to hero figures, and has tremendous energy when activated.

For many of us the hero is asleep, and so we project our hero archetype onto other people around us. So we go to movies, lectures, and concerts looking for heroes. We keep our eyes open for models, constantly hoping to find someone we can trust implicitly, look up to, believe in, and follow. The alternative is to discover that hero reality in ourselves, free its energy to work for us, and become our own heroes.

In my work with dreams, I assume this deeper Jungian understanding of the nature of the human unconscious. I assume that there are deep, mysterious realities alive in us that we need to understand and accept. Pretending they aren't there makes them dangerous to our health. To ignore or deny the archetypes and their influence in our lives is like rowing a boat on the ocean while denying there are such things as sharks, whales, dolphins, and edible fish swimming beneath us.

Like the ocean, the unconscious is a deep and rich resource. Living apart from it leaves us thin, not fully in touch with our whole being. To be a whole person, we need to explore the unconscious, listen to its guidance, open ourselves to its richness, be aware of its dangers. We can never empty the unconscious nor plumb its depths. It is always beyond us, more than we can ever fully comprehend with our finite, conscious mind. And so it is a lifelong task to continue to explore it—learning more, growing in our understanding, though knowing that we will never exhaust its riches.

We may speak, then, of two levels of the unconscious—the layer of the personal unconscious and the deeper or collective layer we all have in common. In our personal unconscious are the memories, traumas, and secrets of our individual lives. In the collective layer are the archetypal realities we share with others but which we still relate to and deal with individually. So my relationship to the hero archetype will be utterly different from yours, and the way it manifests itself in my life will also be different. At the same time, it is present in all of us.

In the deeper unconscious, we find that core reality of acceptance, love, and unconditional okayness that most of us seek all our lives. The existence of the unconscious is not bad news nor a menace, though it sometimes confronts us in a menacing way to get our attention. It is basically good news, deep guidance, and great joy. For God is there waiting for us.

When I work with people in psychotherapy, I operate with the assumption that this deeper unconscious is a tremendous resource in therapy. More importantly, the client has a tremendous ally in his or her own unconscious. So this operating assumption makes a great difference in how I work and how the therapy proceeds.

A second very basic and very important assumption is the reality of the inner self. For thousands of years, various religious systems have had a variety of names for the inner self, a hidden part of us that makes us uniquely human. It may be known as the soul, the Atman, the inner light, or the self. The self, to use Jung's word for it, is a more specifically personal aspect of the deeper unconscious.

A young man I have worked with in therapy may illustrate this reality of the inner self and the unconscious. (He has given me permission to share this very personal story. I have changed his name, of course.) Jim, now in his mid-thirties, came for help in solving the problem of his addictions. He had fallen into the ever-present drug culture of our time and was a regular user of cocaine and alcohol.

In a powerful dream he related to me, Jim saw an Oriental man standing naked beside his bed. He could not understand why the man was there nor what he represented. I suggested to Jim that he try a meditative conversation with the Oriental man, a practice Jung called *active imagination.* Active imagination is a powerful resource we are only beginning to tap, and I will return to discuss its use more fully as we approach the inner teacher in relation to dreams.

I had Jim do some deep breathing, then lie completely relaxed and "go inside." After a few moments he reported that he could see the Oriental man who had appeared in his dream. "Who are you, and why did you come in my dream?" he asked.

"I am the spiritual part of you, and I am very old," he said. Jim began to sob quietly as he heard this. "I am the ancestor of your ancestors. I am older than the American Indians who left my culture and came to this land. I am your soul." The image then changed, and the figure Jim saw appeared as an Indian chief with an eagle on his shoulder. "We are on your side, and it was our guidance that got you to come here for help," said the figure in Jim's unconscious. "We have kept you from getting into more serious trouble than you have." More sobbing. Jim was deeply moved. The figure reassured him: "The trouble you are having now will pass. We are always available to help you when you need us."

Jim had not been accustomed to turning within for help. He had been living superficially, unaware of his unconscious. But from this moment forward, Jim knew that his deeper, inner self was on his side and that as a result he would be more in charge of his own life.

In an equally powerful dream, a woman client of mine reported a vision that could not help but affect her whole life. (Diane—not her real name—also agreed to share her story with others.) In the dream, Diane found herself as an infant in a hospital room. A woman would pick her up, carry her in her arms for a few minutes, then put her down again as though unsure she wanted the child. A man appeared in the doorway of the room but would not come inside. He seemed angry, and the infant could feel his rejection. The scene changed, and the child was in a car with the man and woman driving through a blizzard.

Suddenly, a great storm came and swept the car into the air. Diane found herself falling into the ocean and sinking slowly to the bottom. Soon a fish came and looked at her. This was no ordinary fish. It was large, round, and golden. The fish motioned for Diane to follow it. The fish then led the way to a cave at the bottom of the sea. Inside the hidden cave was an old chest. When Diane opened the chest, she found it filled with gems and treasure. As she left, the fish remained behind to guard the treasure and the cave for her.

In symbolic language, this woman's inner self was assuring her of the deep, inner resources at the very depths of her being. For the rest of her life she will know that there are riches within her that she can count on. In spite of an unhappy childhood and a deep sense of not being wanted, she is rich within herself. The golden fish may be considered a symbol of the self or the soul, and it led her to her marvelous cave deep in the unconscious. Coming at the beginning of her therapy work, Diane's dream was a tremendous help, a sign to her that she could safely explore her inner being and find unknown resources for her life journey. I felt deeply moved and thrilled, as I always do when I meet the deep, inner realities of the human spirit.

There are also times when the exploration of the unconscious does not seem indicated for a particular person. I remember a young woman who came to work on her dreams with me. In our second hour together she told me a dream in which she found herself in an underground cavern. Many of her friends and family were there as well. The ground began to tremble, and bits of rock began to fall from the roof of the cave. People began running in panic. The dreamer left the cave safely as the dream ended. It was my feeling upon hearing this dream that this young woman should not proceed with her exploration of inner matters through dreams. Her dream seemed to me to be a warning against dangerous aspects that should not be pursued. She felt the same way, and we ended our work together. I trust the messages of the unconscious, and they often guide me in my decisions.

Seeing Yourself in Your Dreams

There is a cardinal rule accepted by most dream workers: "Everything in your dream is an aspect of you." If you see a monster in your dream, it represents some part of yourself. If you see a murderer, part of you is murderer, real or potential. I remember saying once to a group of students at Union Theological Seminary in New York that we are all potential murderers. They rebelled at my suggestion with horror and became quite angry. Murderers are some other kind of creature, a different species, a lower order of humanity. Not so. We are all one, and the potential exists in all of us to be anything.

I remember a friend who dreamed that he was in a valley that was parched with drought. People were desperately thirsty, terribly in need of water. Plants and trees were burning up. At the head of the valley stood a dam, and behind the dam, a tremendous body of water. If we apply the cardinal rule to this dream, then my friend was both the parched valley and the dam. I asked him to pretend to be the dam and let it speak. "Ask the dam why it does not water the valley below," I suggested. The dam replied that it held back a tremendous amount of energy from the valley below because it was afraid that if it released the energy it would destroy everything. This suddenly made great sense to my friend, who realized that he was holding back his energy from his work because he was afraid his work would overwhelm him if he devoted full energy to it. Everything in the dream is an aspect of ourselves.

One reason we have trouble accepting our troublesome parts is our polarized belief system inherited from the Greek philosophers. We believe that we are either good people or bad people, good boys/girls or bad. Believing this, we must find everything about ourselves to be good. If we find any bad apples, the whole barrel might be bad, and this would disqualify us from the human race or from getting into heaven. And so many of us live in our false self-image and fiercely defend any suggestion that we are imperfect.

I remember a young woman who came to me for counseling. She had been called on the carpet by her supervisor at work and told that she needed to work on being less defensive. Her response was to be highly indignant and to gather evidence from her co-workers and subordinates to prove to the boss that he was wrong. In other words, she reacted in a highly defensive manner, actually demonstrating that the boss was right. When I tried to show her in her therapy session that the boss might be right and that she indeed might look in the mirror and attempt to understand her own defensive life-style, she quit therapy. She had invested so much in her self-image, in being perfect, that she could not admit that she had any shadow parts.

In contrast, many people who come to learn more about themselves do learn to accept and own their dark sides, admit their imperfections, and accept themselves as deep and mysterious. That is the ideal for personal growth—to accept the imperfections as part of our nature and move toward a greater wholeness.

A very competent professor once dreamed that he had been named manager of a professional baseball team. Since he knew almost nothing about baseball, he felt out of place, inadequate, foolish. I asked him to consider what part of him was this inadequate, out-of-place baseball manager. As a boy, Rob's father had been a "jock," always active in sports. Rob had not been good at sports and had always felt inadequate when forced to participate. He was more artistic and sensitive, traits his macho father feared were sissy and homosexual. In his adult life, though he was competent and admired, Rob had a part of him that still felt inadequate and foolish. Rob now could admit to this "not good enough" part of himself and bring it more into consciousness—which was the purpose of his dream. In so doing, he became more accepting of himself and gave less energy and power to his feelings of inadequacy. Everything in a dream is a part of us, if we can only accept and own it.

I remember the young woman who dreamed there was a sad little girl sitting at her side. I asked her how old the little girl was in the dream. "About three or four" was the answer. And what was happening to you at that age? I asked. "That was about the time we moved, and I had to give up my little friend Susan, who lived next door. We were inseparable." In this woman's family, crying was not allowed, and so her tears, her sadness had been suppressed all those years. She was told it was silly to cry over losing a four-year-old friend; she would meet new friends in her new home. "I never had another friend as close or as important as Susan," she reported. I suggested that perhaps she had made a decision never to let anyone take Susan's place, and so her sadness remained undiminished. "Yes, it was like a tribute to how important she was in my life." "And would you like to let that sadness go now, change that decision?" I asked her. "Yes, I think it's time," she said.

At painful moments we often make decisions that remain with us for the rest of our lives: "I'll never love again"; "I'll never let anyone see my tears again"; "I won't talk back to adults again; it doesn't pay." You may wish to ask yourself what core decisions still affect your life that might well be changed or modified now. And your dreams may remind you of decisions that need reexamination.

Only You Can Interpret Your Dreams

As a therapist, I use dreams consistently as one of the best tools for telling me where a person is in his or her life journey and what that person needs to be working on. It is often tempting to say, "That means you haven't finished working on. . . . " And it is true that I may have a strong feeling about the meaning of a client's dream. It is important for you to know, and for me to remember, that no one can really know the meaning of another's dreams. No matter how well trained we are, we can only offer possible ways of understanding another's dreams. It is the dreamer who must decide whether that offering, that possibility, makes any sense.

After all, how can any therapist or analyst know the full background of your life, the depth of your soul, and the intricacies of your present life? We therapists can know some of this, but you know it far deeper than we ever can.

One way you know a dream interpretation has hit its mark is when some energy moves in you as a result of it. If your solar plexus tightens up, your body jumps, or you feel dizzy, you know something important is happening. I remember offering a dream interpretation to a woman who gasped and moved visibly. I asked her, "What happened just then?" She put one hand at her neck and one at her pelvis and said, "Everything from here to here just turned upside down." On the other hand, if you feel nothing, perhaps the interpretation missed the mark.

The important thing to remember is that you should not accept someone's interpretation of your dream if it does not feel right to you. The fact that someone has a Ph.D. after his or her name or has been stamped "approved" by some professional group does not obligate you to accept everything the person says as gospel.

Strephon Williams, in his interesting book *Jungian-Senoi Dreamwork Manual,* has said:

> One of the central values of dreamwork is developing a relationship to one's own inner authority. Dreams come from within, from one's own sources, and not from some outer authority, however knowledgeable.[1]

Williams, who emphasizes the importance of each person's developing his or her own dreamwork patterns, also stated:

> Don't tell me what my dream means, please. You will only be telling me what my dream means to you, not what it means to me. If you want to help me, give me specific suggestions that I can use to re-experience my own dreams. Then I can learn to rely on my own sources and not be forced to submit to someone else's way of looking at things.[2]

For those who can afford to do so, or are willing to make the necessary sacrifices, working with a competent professional can be a remarkably powerful experience. The danger is that we allow ourselves to become dependent upon the professional to tell us who we are and what our dreams mean. Rather, the goal of such personal growth-oriented therapy should be to free us from dependence, develop our own analytic skills, and help us to trust our deep, intuitive inner resources. We may need to begin with a professional dreamworker, then wean ourselves.

You already know what is best for you and your life. Trust that inner knowing, and act on it.

Notes

1. Strephon Kaplan Williams, *Jungian-Senoi Dreamwork Manual* (Berkeley: Journey Press, 1980), p. 26.
2. Ibid., p. 15.

3

COMMITMENT TO YOUR INNER SELF

To really learn from your dreams, you must first make a commitment to your inner journey. You must affirm the prime importance of your inner self and the utterly different world it represents. Carl Jung has pointed out that the psychology of the second half of life is a wholly different psychology from that of the first half. In roughly the first 35 years of life, we are concerned with establishing ourselves in the world—building a career, finding a mate, beginning a family, accumulating possessions. Then in the succeeding years we tend to turn to different issues and ask different questions.

In the second half of life we begin to ask questions such as these:
- What is my life all about?
- Who am I really?
- What should I be doing with the rest of my life, my energy?

It is in the second half's journey that we begin to look inside, make contact with our unconscious, listen to our inner self. Dreams are an excellent way to further this journey, though there are many other ways as well.

Many people find it difficult to make this basic commitment to the inner self, the soul. The pervasive concern for security raises its ugly head and hinders the inner search. The most common fears that block this important growth are:
- If I listen to my inner self, how do I know it's real and not just a figment of my imagination?

- My inner self may ask me to make changes I am unwilling to make.
- I know I should clean up my life, leave my marriage, change my destructive life patterns, but it would be painful; my parents wouldn't approve, my friends would be upset.

Trying to avoid pain is a very common deterrent to growth. What many such persons often fail to recognize and admit is that there is also pain in refusing to grow. To stagnate, to go stale on life, to die spiritually is painful, too. Sometimes it is just a matter of choosing which pain we prefer.

Often we see bitter people who have ignored the call of the unconscious and hardened their spirits against the deeper inner life. But it is dangerous to go on with business as usual in the second half of life. Something dies inside us. Life becomes a bore. Success loses its savor, and the creative fires burn low. So making a commitment is important, even crucial, to our happiness and fulfillment; it is perhaps a life-or-death choice. To make such a commitment means spending time, energy, and money in the pursuit of self-knowledge and spiritual growth.

"But I can't afford it! I'm barely getting by now," we cry in response. And the words of Jesus of Nazareth come back to us, "For where your treasure is, there will your heart be also" (Matthew 6:21). When we set our hearts on a new car, we find a way to work out the financing. When we want a vacation in Mexico, we locate the money somewhere or borrow it from our mother's trust fund. When we are ready to make a similar commitment to our own growth, we are following the flow of the unconscious, and energy begins to move within us.

People often ask me, "But what if I can't remember my dreams?" Many people do not remember their dreams, though dream research has demonstrated that we all dream nightly. And there are many reasons why we may have shut off our dreams and do not remember them, many reasons why the flow or dialogue between the conscious self and the unconscious is impeded. I remember one man who told me he had a frightening dream when he was a small boy, and he swore he would never dream again. He has not remembered one dream since.

I also believe that some people do not need their dreams as a way of listening to the inner self. Some persons are in more direct communication with the inner self. They live more simply and closer to the unconscious; they do not need nighttime to open the communication. I believe these persons are rare, but they do exist.

If you do not remember your dreams and wish to begin doing so, start by purchasing a notebook or journal in which to write your dreams. Honor your dreams by spending enough money to get an attractive, inviting book that says your dreams are important.

Next, place the journal and a pen or pencil by your bedside. As you go to bed, earnestly ask your unconscious to send you a dream and to help you to remember it. However, if you do not intend to spend adequate time with your dreams, honoring them with writing and reflection time, making that basic commitment, then don't start. But don't expect much.

Some people find it helpful to place a tape recorder beside their bed and talk the dream into it if they awaken during the night with a dream memory. I recall suggesting that to one of my clients in therapy. But I asked that she write the dream down and bring along the written, edited version to her counseling sessions with me. Instead, she would grab the tape recorder, which she had not bothered to listen to, and begin playing it in my office. We would hear this squawky, sleepy, mumbling voice, barely audible—and the client couldn't understand it herself. It was a waste of her time with me. I would repeat my request that she write down her dream before coming, but her commitment was so low that she continued to bring the unedited, unhelpful tape, which I finally refused to allow. Moral of this story: If you do use a tape recorder during the night so as not to awaken your partner by turning on a light (or for some other reason), please honor the dreams enough to write down the message the next day.

Sometimes as we wake up we remember little or nothing of the dream. However, if we take our pen in hand anyway and begin to write, the dream *can* return to mind. If you remember only a fragment, write at least that fragment. Even a fragment can be useful and revealing in the hands of a skilled helper. And writing a little may bring more of the memory to the surface.

Occasionally, nothing seems to work. You can have the commitment, the notebook, the desire, and still remember nothing. I remember a friend who attended a workshop on dreams I offered one summer. She was deeply interested in dreams, but she seemed unable to remember a single one. Surely, she thought, if she traveled several hundred miles to attend a dreams workshop, she would begin to remember. The stimulation of the lectures and the discussion of dreams would cause her to begin remembering. But, alas, even the conference did not help. Day after day went by, and still she had not remembered a single dream.

On her last night, she remembered that someone had suggested setting an alarm clock for the middle of the night, waking up, and writing down the dream you were just having. (This can work if the timing is just right.) So Ellen set her alarm for 3 A.M. and fell fast asleep. At the appointed hour, she was awakened by the loud clanging of her alarm, sat bolt-upright in bed, was frightened half to death (unable to remember anything), and could not get back to sleep the rest of the night! So her alarm clock experiment was a total failure, and she returned home dreamless. If you are unable to remember your dreams even though you want to and do try, do not feel badly. Do not blame yourself or put yourself down. Simply use other methods for your inner growth, and wait.

If you have never had any exposure to dreamwork, you may find it valuable to attend a workshop or class on it, or you may want to find an authority to help you get started. I would not recommend therapists who are trained in classical

Freudian psychology for an introduction to dreamwork. They tend to stress sexual interpretations too heavily, since that was the bias of Freud himself. A Jungian analyst or a therapist with solid Jungian training would be best. See the section of suggested readings on p. 107 for additional help, but remember that a personal experience can help the information in books come alive.

One more point. Here is a basic rule of thumb for dream interpretation: *Dreams have their meaning within the context of your daily life!* This is not an absolute rule; there are exceptions, I'm sure. Most of the time, however, it will hold true. Dreams are basically your individual property. They belong to you and have meaning in relation to your own life. Your dreamworld is not a separate world of fantastic imagery that is entirely apart from you and your everyday living. You and your dreamworld form one world. They are *one piece*. This holistic attitude is essential, for it will keep you from reading your dreams in utterly irrelevant ways.

Because dreams and daily life are so closely related, two persons having the same dream on the same night may find entirely different meanings in those dreams. Your friend dreaming the same dream has a different set of circumstances operating, and the dream stems from an entirely different personal history. In a recent workshop, two women worked on dreams in which they were holding a new baby. Both women were past the age when it is ideal to bear children, so we had to ask, "What is the meaning of this image of a child in your life?"

For one of the women, it was clear that some new birth was ready in her life. It had its meaning in the context of her life—a readiness for rebirth, new life, a new chapter for her. The birth of an infant in a dream is usually related to some new energy in one's life. Hence it is usually a significant event to dream of a new child.

For the second woman, the child meant something entirely different. The context of her life made a great difference in the interpretation. In her background was a very close relationship with her father. As she reached puberty, her father pulled away. She had been angry about that ever since—a common story for young women. The deep unconscious desire for a young girl to have her father for herself was still alive in her unconscious. The child was really an offering to her father, and the dream tipped her off that it was time to let go of the childhood fantasy that her father could be her "man." As she acted to let go of her father, she experienced a deep sense of relief and a freedom she had never known. She could now give up reacting to men through the hidden screen of that desire for her father. The context of her life, then, made a great difference in how she understood the infant in her dream.

Occasionally a person will have a dream that does not seem related to everyday life but seems to cut across daily routines or explode them. These are the rare "archetypal dreams" or "big dreams" that erupt from a deeper, communal level of the unconscious and call our attention to something bigger and more important than daily life. Even here, however, our lack of openness to growth may cause or trigger the "big dream." In most instances, I look to the context of the dreamer's life for the meaning of the dream. We can ask questions such as:

- What was going on in my life at the time of this dream?
- How is this dream related to the questions I am asking currently, or the issues I am wrestling with?
- Is this dream relevant to the decision I am struggling with now?

If we look for such connections, we can usually discover the crucial relationship between the dream and what is going on in our lives.

4

UNLOCKING YOUR OWN DREAMS

A unique feature of this book is that it offers the average person a simple way to approach his or her dreams. As I looked over the current literature on dreams, my overall impression was, "Wow! So where do I begin?" Many of the books on dreams seem terribly complex—and the subject of dreams *is* terribly complex! I have written this book for those persons who are not ready to tackle all the deeper dimensions of dream theory but who want some ways to begin. One way to approach dreams simply yet profoundly is through a series of questions. I offer such a series of questions in this chapter, with some discussion of each, as basic approaches to your own dreamwork.

If you were working on your dreams with a trained Jungian analyst, you might be asked these very questions. Indeed, I have been. But you can ask yourself the same questions and gain some benefit from the answers, though you do not have the training, background, and intuitive expertise of the analyst present. If you can work with your own dreams *and* with an analyst, so much the better. But if you cannot afford an analyst or do not have one within reach, the following questions can get you started.

At the end of this book, on p. 104, you will find a dream-journal form based on the series of questions presented in the following chapter. You may copy it (without written permission) for your individual use. Even better yet, begin with this form and revise it to reflect your particular needs and interests. We must request that you note on any quantity that you reproduce the source from which it came, including author, title, and publisher. Remember to include this information if you duplicate a quantity for your own daily use or for an informal dream group.

You will notice that the dream-journal form begins by asking you to date your dream and give it a title. Dating your dreams is important. Because the dream is so often related to your life context, it is important to record the date *and* the important events taking place in your life at that time. I always record the date of the morning I write the dream in my journal, so the dates are consistent. Some prefer to record the date from the night before. But what if the dream occurs after midnight? The dating of the dream does not matter as long as your method is basically consistent. Dr. Edith Wallace suggests dating the dream in dual numbers (for example, January 12/13) to represent the night before and the morning after the dream.

I (and many others) find it valuable to give the dream a title, just as in a book or movie. Titling the dream brings out one important element, the motif.

Importance of Motif, Detail, and Context

The motif is the theme or the thread that runs through the dream or series of dreams. We usually need to step back and look at the dream as a whole to determine the motif. This process of distancing ourselves from dreams is valuable in that it places us in an objective position and hence offers a more neutral look at the material. For instance, as we step back and look at three dreams from last night, we may find a common note in what at first appears to be three very different activities. We may, for example, be able to see that all three dreams deal with sexuality. Or we may find that in all three we are running away from something. When the motif is clear, we can then ask, "Okay, then, what is it in my life I am running away from? And do I want to continue running from it? Can I now choose to confront it and deal with it in a new way?"

Just discovering the motif of the dream or series of dreams may be all you need to understand it more fully. If running away is the motif, then you need to look at how you are running away, from what, for what reason, and what to do about it next. That may be the primary point of the dream: to call your attention to your pattern of running from something (or everything) of importance. Examining other aspects of the dream and doing a finer, point-by-point analysis can also be helpful, but on occasion the motif is all you need.

When you keep a dream journal over a period of time, you can look back and study how often that theme comes up, how your dealings with it have changed, and where you stand with it now. A friend recently remarked, "My dream journal is the most interesting book I know; it is fascinating to study the themes and how they have changed over the past three years."

If you feel that the title of your dream (or the series of dreams from that night) does not really capture the motif, then note the motif as well (perhaps written under the title). You will find that this can be very useful information.

The next important step in recording your dream is writing down the dream in detail. Some people like to reach for their pen and book immediately upon awakening. I prefer to make a brief note or two, then come back to the detailed writing after I shower, dress, and meditate for a time. It's like securing your boat to the wharf with a tie line so it won't drift away. You will need to find the pattern that works best for you.

I suggest that you write the dream as though you were still actually *in* the dream. Write in the present tense rather than the past tense, so that you keep the dream material alive rather than distancing it by making it already past: "I am standing on the bridge looking down at the water." This form has more power than "I was standing on the bridge. . . . "

As you write the dream, remember to record every detail you can recall. Was it night, or day? Was the sun shining?

What color was the person's clothing? How did you feel when the "thing" approached? Were you wearing unusual clothes? Were there other people present? Did you recognize any of them? It may also be important to note what period of history the dream is set in. Are the costumes modern, primitive, Elizabethan?

Sometimes we disdain seemingly insignificant dream fragments. I occasionally ask clients in a therapy session, "And did you have any dreams last night?" They sometimes reply, "Oh, just a fragment that didn't mean anything." I usually ask them to tell me the fragment and let me decide with them whether or not it has meaning.

I remember a well-known doctor who once told me his dream was nothing but a fragment. I asked him to tell me the fragment anyway. All he could recall was a hand throwing his billfold out on the table in front of him. So I asked him to do that very thing, to throw his billfold on the coffee table in my office. I then asked him what it represented to him. How would it be if he left without his billfold? He thought about it and realized that he could not drive his car, purchase anything, or prove who he was.

In short, a great deal of his identity was wrapped up in that billfold. And so the motif of personal identity was raised by an innocent and barely remembered dream fragment. He and I took a serious look at his personal crisis—a concern about who he really was behind the facade of his profession. This proved to be a crucially important issue for him. The fact that only a fragment of the dream was remembered possibly highlighted the identity issue more than a whole series of dreams could have done. The fragment drew attention to the issue, just as putting the beam of a powerful flashlight on an object would do. So when you are tempted to dismiss a dream image, thought, or fragment as unimportant, play with it anyway. It may be a gem in the rough.

The next item on the dream-journal form deals with the importance of the context of the dream.

Context and its relationship to dreams has been discussed in the previous chapter. The meaning of the dream is nearly always related to what is happening (or not happening that ought to be) in our everyday life. So it is important to note any outstanding events or influences. You may record items such as:

- "My sister called last night to tell me our mother is seriously ill."
- "My supervisor told me yesterday that he wanted to see me in his office this morning. I feel old insecurities coming up as I worry about what he wants to tell me."
- "I am feeling bored with life lately, stuck, no enthusiasm."

Earlier in this book I noted the tendency to deal with a dream as a separate entity in itself, as though it were a message from outer space with no connection to daily existence. Remember that the more sensible approach is to listen to the dream as a message from the inner self which addresses you as a total person living in this world and struggling with its everyday issues.

Persons in the Dream

The persons who appear in your dreams are significant to you for several reasons: They represent important issues or realities in your psyche, and they can be powerfully instructive when examined more closely. Since it is assumed that there are many "selves" within us, that we are a number of "personalities," a combination of qualities, these qualities can show up through the persons in our dreams.

Perhaps the best illustration of this point is to share with you some of the personal qualities that make up my own personality. I have already indicated that I have within me an arrogant, self-righteous so-and-so that sometimes gets in my way. I also have within me, lying around in my unconscious somewhere, a hurting boy-child. This boy part did not feel fully accepted and was shy and lonely at times. He still surfaces occasionally. There is also within me a caring, nurturing self that reaches out with warmth and love to my children and others I know. Many selves coexist within me, and the way to know myself more deeply is to get acquainted with all of them—in all their richness and their drawbacks. The fear that we may find unacceptable selves within us holds many people back from looking at their dreams. Take courage and plunge ahead, for this move will only help you to become more whole. Know that there is within you (as within others) the seductress (or seducer), the witch (or wizard), the artist, and the poet. Embrace all these disparate parts and you will be the richer for it.

We must make an important decision when we come to examine the person or persons in our dreams: Are we going to view the person objectively, or subjectively? If you actually know the person and he or she is beating you over the head in the dream, perhaps that person really is harming or bullying you in some way. Such a view would be an objective interpretation. You decide by testing it: Is Bill actually beating me in a way that I must now look at more closely? If Bill lives in South America and has no contact with you that could be considered as beating or bullying, then you know the meaning is subjective or symbolic. The question then is different: What *is* beating me on the head, and how can I understand this "Bill" figure in the dream?

Interpreting known persons

The methods we use to interpret the meaning of known persons in a dream are different from the ones we use with unknown persons. So it is vital to make that distinction as you reflect on the dream. The dream-journal form asks you to consider who are the main characters who are known to you in the dream; you also need to evaluate the outstanding characteristics of these characters and the part of you that the characters may represent.

One of my own dreams relates to this subject. About five years ago I dreamed of an old grade-school classmate. In fact, I dreamed of Tommy twice in one week. I felt this was very unusual, because I had never been close to Tommy and I had not contacted him in the forty years since leaving that school. I was curious about why he would turn up in my dreams. I asked myself: "What were Tommy's outstanding characteristics?"

The answer came immediately. Tommy's primary quality was that he was a very sensitive kid. In fact, he was famous as the school "crybaby"; he would cry if you looked at him the wrong way. The next question I found very uncomfortable: "And what part of me does this person represent?" I twisted and writhed as I pondered my answer. What part of me is the crybaby? I also realized that the answer had something to do with grade-school days, since that was the time the dreammaker had chosen.

When I was in grade school, I too was very sensitive. But I held my feelings inside, did not entrust them to my schoolmates. I felt alone a great deal of the time, but I put a mask on my feelings and cried inside. My older brother taught me how to box, how to lead with my left jab, keep my chin down, and protect myself. When someone picked a fight with me, then, he usually regretted it. In short, my reaction to being sensitive was to protect myself with armor and present a fighter-response to my pain. Tommy's reaction was to release his pain in tears.

That summer, five years ago, I did a lot of crying. I discovered many old, repressed tears in me (the Tommy part of me), and I chose to let them flow. I would cry easily and it felt good to release my tears. That simple dream of an old schoolmate helped open up parts of me that had been guarded for years—too many years.

The material I've revealed about Tommy illustrates how to use other persons in your dreams to learn about your many "selves." If I had haughtily dismissed the "crybaby" as "not me," I would have bypassed an important growth opportunity. Owning that "crybaby" part of me did not make me a weakling. Rather, it made me stronger as I released old energy that had been pent up for years.

How did this crying period connect with the context of my life? That summer had been painful—I had felt more alone and abandoned than in a long time, so the crying was both current and ancient. This experience helped me see that my loneliness and hurt feelings had deep roots in my childhood that I had been ignoring.

This one question, concerning known persons in your dreams, can help you unlock many dreams and reveal numerous parts of yourself. Sometimes the part of you represented by the person in the dream will be obscure or unacceptable. At other times the meaning becomes clear only after you do active imagination with the person or figure, closing both eyes and having a dialogue with that person's image. (Active imagination will be discussed further in Chapter 7.)

An excellent way to discover the salient characteristics of the known person in a dream is to write down five adjectives that describe that person. Then see if one of the adjectives fits you. For example, it may be that a friend in a dream is basically psychic and represents the psychic part of you which you tend to deny or repress. Or the friend may be an exceptionally strong person who represents your inner strength.

Interpreting unknown persons

Jung's concept of the shadow was one of his great contributions to the world of psychology. Every human has a dark or hidden side to his or her nature, according to Jung. Our task in life is to bring more and more of that hidden part into the light, or into consciousness. The shadow is not a theoretical formulation he made up to explain something. The shadow is a reality in the human psyche that manifests itself in a variety of ways. Jung experienced his own shadow and then helped numerous clients to recognize and deal with theirs.

When we see in our dreams a person of our same sex whom we do not recognize, there is a good chance it is this shadow part of us surfacing, an element that we need to know. So the third question on the dream-journal form asks you to list the main characters in the dream who are not known to you, specifiying those who are of your same sex.

The accepted theory for followers of Jung's thought is that the shadow usually presents itself as an unknown person of the same sex as the dreamer. I say *usually* because I believe there are exceptions, especially when the shadow archetype in the unconscious is fused with an opposite-sex archetype and they appear as one figure. For example, if a woman has had bad experiences with men, male figures may appear in shadowy form, fusing the opposite-sex and shadow archetypes. Jungians usually speak of the shadow as of the same sex, however, and I have heard well-known lecturers say this is always so. I happen to believe that there is only one absolute in dealing with the unconscious: that there are *no* absolutes. There are general tendencies, rules of thumb, but I doubt there are any unbreakable rules about something as rich, deep, and mysterious as the human unconscious.

It is not my intention in this book to discuss (in great detail) a subject as deep and vast as the shadow. For more thorough discussion of this concept, I suggest you turn to Jung's writings or to other books in the suggested reading list on p. 107. I will only offer a few illustrations of how the shadow manifests itself in dreams and how we might relate to it.

I once led a dream workshop in Canada in which an earnest young man told the following dream. He dreamed that he had gone down the stairs into his basement and found a great, dark shadow in the far corner. He could sense that it was evil, an enemy, and he was very frightened. He fled the basement and closed the door that led to the stairs.

We discussed the dream. The dreamer told me that he knew he must someday return to the basement and destroy that evil thing. I suggested a different approach, saying that he needed to go back into the basement and confront the being. Perhaps he should talk to it and find out why it had come into his dream, why it seemed so dark and evil to him. I reminded him that everything in the dream was a part of himself, that he needed to know and accept it, rather than kill it. I knew that the dreamer was a very nice man, an individual who had tried to please everybody throughout his life. That meant he allowed no anger or unpleasantness, and it was my hunch that his "evil" shadow was—or could be— his own suppressed anger. I asked him if he would be willing to explore the dream further, and he replied that he would.

I then asked the dreamer to close his eyes and take some deep breaths. When he seemed quite relaxed and centered, I proposed that he see himself returning to the basement to talk with the shadow. He reported that he was descending the stairs and could see the shadow back in the corner. "I'm going to kill you," he called out to the shadow. I said, "Wait a minute! You can't kill a part of yourself. You have to come to terms with it. Try talking to it."

The dreamer called out, "Who are you, and what are you doing in my basement?" The shadow did not reply in words, but began to shrink and to appear less ominous, more gray. The dreamer began to feel less afraid. On that occasion, that was all he accomplished. The "evil" presence did not now seem so threatening, and I proposed that he return to the basement in his imagination when he felt ready to get better acquainted with his shadow. This example demonstrates an almost classic shadow dream.

One of the problems in dealing with shadow material is that we are conditioned to regard anything unknown as alien, threatening, and possibly evil. The shadow part of us is not evil, not against us, unless we make it an enemy by our attitude toward it, as did the dreamer with the "thing" in his basement. In fact, the energy of the shadow can work with us if we only allow it to. But when we repress unacceptable parts of ourselves such as our anger, then it can truly become an enemy and work against our best interests.

Let me share with you a dream that illustrates the positive dimension of the shadow in us. I once dreamed that I was in a strange city where I was to meet some friends. I had been advised to go to the top of the hill in the middle of the city to see the view. I had time before my friends were to arrive, so I ascended the hill. In the distance I could see a beautiful mountain. As I prepared to return to the city below, I realized that I had come up the hill in a rowboat. (Don't ask me how a rowboat can go uphill, and on land!) I started back to my rowboat but watched in amazement as a dark man wearing no shirt stepped into the boat before I could. "Just a minute. That's my rowboat," I said to him. "Oh, that's all right. I'll row for you," he said.

This strong, dark man was my shadow and also my ally. After years of working at getting to know my shadow, this dream reassured me that "he" was with me, ready to help me with his strength. When I find myself short of energy, I often envision that shirtless man rowing in the boat with me, and my strength is more than the strength of one. This dream indicates the power of a positive shadow dream.

By considering the unknown same-sex persons in our dreams to be ourselves, and especially by engaging them in dialogue, we can get to know our shadow a little at a time. We never exhaust this shadow, and we never get it all into the light. All human beings have a shadow, and so we will always find a part of us unknown and hidden, a mystery. Our lifelong task is to continue the effort to know the shadow, though we will never complete the job.

Our shadow, then, can be very positive; it is not necessarily bad. Hidden in us reside tremendous resources—personal gifts, talents, creativity, strength, and beauty—that we have not suspected. When we can stop regarding the shadow as our enemy and look at both its dark, scary aspects and its rich gifts, we are indeed growing as persons.

The next question on the dream-journal form is also about unknown characters in dreams, specifically those persons who are of the opposite sex. We will now consider those unknown figures who are not of the same sex as ourselves.

Opposite-sex dream figures
Every man carries within him an inner feminine self, which Jung calls the *anima*. Every woman carries in her psyche an opposite-sex figure, which Jung calls the *animus*. These inner figures are of tremendous importance and represent

one of the most crucial contributions Jung made to modern psychology, although other psychologies still strangely pay no attention to this basic human reality. If you wish to pursue this complex issue, turn to the suggested readings on p. 107. In this book, I will limit myself to a brief discussion of these figures, how they show up in dreams, and how they affect our lives.

No human being is purely masculine or feminine. Each person includes both qualities, though most are clearly either men or women in their essence. As a man, for instance, I am certain that I have a feminine self. At times, in doing my work as a therapist, I know I am working through the masculine side of my personality. At other times, that simply is inappropriate, and I am sure that I am using more of the feminine. To illustrate, on one occasion I was leading a group of clergy in an evening discussion at a growth center. One of the men had clearly had too much wine before supper, and he was becoming obnoxious, rudely interrupting and dominating the discussion. I tried reasoning with him, to no avail. Finally, I brought my fist down on the table with a great crash. "That's enough," I cried, paralyzing the startled clergy around the table. "Go to your room and sleep it off, and when you have sobered up, you can come back and join us." It was strongly authoritarian behavior, coming from the masculine side of my being. The man struggled to his feet, looking aghast, and fled the room. Some members of the group were surprised at my behavior, and we discussed why I had felt it appropriate and necessary.

The next morning, the shamefaced fellow asked to speak with me. He apologized for his behavior and thanked me for helping him to get control of himself. He had been unable to gain control of his own actions and appreciated my taking charge. From his point of view, my conduct had been most appropriate, though it appeared rude and aggressive to others.

On another occasion I was talking with a young man about his personal problems, and he was having great difficulty verbalizing what he needed to talk about. His words were coming slowly and with difficulty, and they had no energy in them. He was a strong young man who worked for a construction crew. I could feel we were getting nowhere.

I asked the man to lie down on the floor with his head on a pillow and to close his eyes. I placed my hand on the top of his head and said, "I know how painful this is for you." This gentle, more feminine approach opened the floodgates. The sobs poured from him, and then he could talk freely about his pain. I knew I was working through the feminine side of my psyche to reach this macho young man.

When a man ignores his feminine self, his *anima*, and tries to be wholly masculine, he is only half a man. He has shut off the other half of himself, thinking that doing so makes him a man. But this move only makes him an unfeeling, un-whole man. Unfortunately, such a man often seeks out a woman who is equally out of touch with her animus for a mate, thus resulting in a union of two half-persons. In addition, his anima may become jealous and angry at being ignored and may foul up his relationships with flesh-and-blood women. We men find it hard to relate to "outer women" if we do not tend to the inner woman. We need our anima for many reasons, not the least of which is to help us know how to relate to real women in our lives.

When I devote some time and energy to maintaining my relationship with my inner feminine and allow her space in my life, I am a more complete man and feel better about who I am. Allowing the feminine has nothing to do with being a "sissy" or a weak man. To the contrary, it gives us added dimension as men. All of the above may be said in reverse for women. The relation to the animus provides a kind of inner strength that is the birthright of every woman (it does not just belong to men). Women who live without it are missing something essential to their wholeness.

How does the inner feminine, the anima, show up in a man's dreams? In my experience, the anima wears many masks in my dreams. She comes at times as wife or companion. One figure is a serene nun who walks with me in the garden and discusses lofty matters. Other times, the anima is a seductress, interested only in sex. She may also be a witch or an earthy peasant woman. All aspects of woman are in the anima, and she may take any of those forms, or other forms. As we pay attention to her, she begins to assume a more consistent form, however, and appears as our inner friend, lover, and support. The animus comes, similarly, in many masculine forms. Behind those masks of the athlete, warrior, sadist, and priest is the inner lover, the inner mate.

John, a man I know, dreamed that he and a male friend walked into an apartment with a woman he did not recognize. The woman walked up behind the male friend, rubbed her hand on his back between the shoulder blades, and plunged a knife into him. In a rage, the dreamer picked the woman up and threw her down the stairs. The dream upset my gentle friend a good deal. I suggested that he needed to discuss the matter with the woman in the dream, to learn why she was so angry that she would murder. If every part of the dream is indeed a part of us, then he needed to know who she was.

So John closed his eyes and went back, in imagination, to the scene of the crime. The woman reappeared. He felt anger again and was about to toss her down the stairs a second time. She spoke: "What the hell are you doing? That part of you I stabbed has been my enemy for years—that dry, pedantic S.O.B. I've loved you all those years. I've known you, wanted you. Now that you've admitted I'm here, let's see how you deal with me."

John replied, "Did you have to kill him?"

She responded: "The so-and-so has got to be dead. (Her eyes are flashing and she is crying.) I love you deeply. I know all about you, all about your shortcomings, all your secret thoughts. I totally accept you. But you have let that logical, intellectual b___ come between you and me and other people. It's been a mask. You can't ignore me any longer. We'll be lovers. You can only use the gifts God gave you with me, so don't fight it."

John embraces her. She is trembling. John can feel her

tears on his face. The hostile anima was softening. John was listening at last, and she was responding with love. This remarkable dialogue was one of the most powerful anima encounters I have ever experienced.

When he opened his eyes again, John suddenly had a revelation. "My God," he said. "That's exactly what Joan's been saying to me for years, and I never understood what she meant." John had been living in an intellectual "man's world" that his wife (Joan) rarely felt, heard, or understood. As he began to listen to his inner woman, his marriage relationship showed improvement as well.

In an introductory book such as this one, I do not pretend to deal with the deeper aspects of this important theme. I urge you to read more deeply, to learn more about this rich material for understanding ourselves. In the meantime, you may ask yourself several related questions:

• Could this opposite-sex figure in my dream be my anima/animus?
• What stands out about him/her?
• What aspect of my anima/animus is represented here?
• What could he/she be saying to me in this dream?

Until you can explore some of the deeper ramifications of Jung's anima/animus theory, these questions will at least give you a start in relating to these important figures as they occur in your dreams.

We have been discussing some of the insights represented by the persons who appear in our dreams. Now we will also examine other aspects of the dream, such as events, interesting features, and symbols. The dream-journal form asks you to list these aspects and consider what part of you is represented by these features.

Whenever something stands out in a dream or is terribly out of place, we usually find it has special meaning. I remember hearing a dream in which the dreamer saw a waterfall in the middle of a church sanctuary. Now that was definitely out of place! We must learn to ask the meaning of such unusual images. Images with great energy, such as tornadoes, earthquakes, or lightning, are dramatic efforts by our unconscious to rattle our cage, get our attention.

In one such dream a jet airliner crashed into the sea and exploded near the dreamer. He needed to ask questions such as "What is about to crash in my life? What danger is near? What needs to end now?"

Another dreamer reported an atomic bomb going off a few miles away. She and her friends and family were safe in a shelter and were not injured. What could that explosion represent? What did it mean that so much energy was being released from her unconscious? And was it good that she was safe, shielded from the consequences?

There are no absolute rules for the meanings of these strong images in our dreams. One of the curses of our humanity is that we always want easy answers. So we turn to incredibly inane sources promising "1,000,000 dream interpretations." Look up "bomb" in such a source and it says, "When you dream of a bomb, it means that your mother-in-law is coming next week." I can say categorically that no such reference can tell you what your dream means. This approach to dreams is usually bereft of basic scholarship and cannot know the individual context of your life, which is crucial in the interpretation of your dreams.

The crucial point remains that the meaning of events such as a flood or explosion in your dreams always lies within you. What is happening in your life? What needs to happen? What danger is close? What is breaking through from your unconscious? Asking questions such as these and listening within for the answers leads you to many exciting dream meanings.

5

SYMBOLS AND ARCHETYPES

In 1972 I went to Zurich, Switzerland, to spend some time exploring the C. G. Jung Institute. In my work with small groups, I had noticed how people would, on occasion, see images from the unconscious, and I wanted to know more about these mental pictures. While attending lectures and getting acquainted, I had a few sessions with Dr. Dieter Baumann, a noted Zurich analyst and Dr. Jung's grandson. I talked with Dr. Baumann about an image I had seen in a dream, a whirling spiral of light, like a whirlpool. He became quite excited. It was my first experience exploring the meaning of a symbol.

If you investigate the symbol of the spiral, you will find that the image is very ancient, complex, and widely known. We see it in the heavens in the spiral nebulae of the stars. The symbol is universally found in ornamental art on buildings. Sources refer to it as an image of the evolution of the universe.[1] From ancient times the spiral has been seen as creative when found in a clockwise direction and destructive when found in a counter-clockwise direction, as in a tornado.

There is also a spiritual dimension to the spiral. As Cirlot comments:

> For the spiral is associated with the idea of the dance, and especially with primitive dances of healing and incantation, when the pattern of movement develops as a spiral curve. Such spiral movements (closely related to the pattern of the mandala and to the spiral form that appears so frequently in art . . .) may be regarded as figures intended to induce a state of ecstasy and to enable man to escape from the material world and to

enter the beyond, through the "hole" symbolized by the mystic Centre.[2]

So what did this spiral image in my dreams have to do with me and my life? I felt the spiral was calling me to a deeper connection with my inner world, the world of the deeper self and of the spiritual. Some people can live their lives on the material plane alone. I cannot. I must live on two planes at once, taking account of the spiritual realm as the foundation of all life.

In meditation one day, long after my sessions with Dr. Baumann, I saw a great spiral of light and shadow whirling down into a central point. In a sudden burst of inspiration, I flung myself (in imagination) into the void, down into the center of the spiral. Instantly, I found myself lying cradled in a great hand, which felt like the hand of God. I remember the words of the biblical poet Job, who spoke of the Lord, "in whose hand is the soul of every living thing, and the breath of all mankind" (Job 12:10).

It is my personal conviction that the inner world, the world of the unconscious, does not belong to psychologists alone. It is the realm of the spirit, the place of healing energy, the abode of God's spirit within us. When I work with people as a pastoral psychotherapist, I am helping them to be in touch with their soul. The spiral image in my dream and in my meditation, then, was a reminder and a bridge between these two essential dimensions of the human person. It was a moving and precious moment—one I will never forget.

It is important to know about symbols and how they can help us understand our dreams. Symbolism may be thought of as the language devised by the unconscious to communicate with the conscious self. In the previous chapter we examined human symbols. Here we are looking at not only abstract symbols such as the circle, square, and spiral, but also animal forms and other images that commonly appear in dreams.

This is not a scholarly discussion of symbols and their place in psychology. Those interested can find a number of excellent books on this important theme (see p. 107). Rather, in an effort to help you work more effectively with your own symbols, I will illustrate some ways to relate to symbols as they appear in dreams. I prefer to give you a feel for how to relate to symbols in your own dreams, rather than give you an intellectual treatment of symbolism in dreams.

One time I was presenting a lecture workshop on dreams in Texas, when a woman in the back row raised her hand to ask a question. "A friend of mine once dreamed that a snake was chasing her," she said. "What would that mean?" "There is no absolute meaning," I replied. "It would depend upon the context—what is happening in that person's life. Since she isn't here to discuss it with us, we'd better stay with the people who are."

When the group took a break for coffee, the woman approached me and said in a low voice, "I was the one who dreamed the snake was chasing me. Could you tell me what it means?" Here I was confronted with a most widespread symbol—the snake. Symbols do have some universal meanings, discussed at length in a scholarly book such as J. E. Cirlot's *Dictionary of Symbols*. Most Jungian analysts have a copy of Cirlot, and the book is widely available. If you look up *snake* in a symbol dictionary, you will find five pages in fine print discussing the many ways in which snakes have been understood in various cultures. Researching a dream symbol can be a fascinating education in itself!

When the lady asked me about her snake, I offered some of those basic and universal meanings to see if any of them fit her. Usually if a dream interpretation connects with us, we will feel some energy move, some connection inside us. I mentioned that the snake can be symbolic of psychic energy itself or of sexual energy *(libido)*. I watched her face and body for responses as I offered other possibilities, such as the fact that the snake's shedding of skin can represent a metamorphosis or life transformation. She did not twitch, jump, cringe, or develop a tic. She simply shook her head no. I went on. In ancient Greek mythology, the snake is related to the god of healing, Aesculapius, whose symbol of a staff with the snake entwined is often associated with medical societies today. Still she shook her head.

Finally, with people all around munching donuts and downing coffee, I asked her to close her eyes and take some deep breaths. "Now go back into the dream and see your snake again." She nodded that she could indeed see the snake. Suddenly, she opened her eyes and said, "I know what my dream means!" She held up her hand coiled like the head of a poised cobra. "I lash out at people," she said, and walked off sadly.

Symbols: Universal and Individual

This woman's experience illustrates how symbols have both universal and individual meaning. There are qualities of snakes which are understandable in every culture. And yet we cannot pick up a dream-interpretation book in the drug store, look up the simplistic meaning of a snake dream, and come up with any sense—only nonsense. The universal meanings must be placed in the context of the individual dreamer's life.

The woman just mentioned had a dream that focused on one dimension of snakes—their propensity to lash out. And look how that dream was related to her life. Running from the pursuing snake signified her desire to avoid facing that uncomplimentary and possibly destructive aspect of her personality. Another common response is to project that lashing snake on friends or family and blame them for being nasty. The moment she admitted, "I lash out at people," her problem was on the table and potentially less dangerous to her and others. She could then choose to work on that undesirable trait and stay conscious of it.

On the dream-journal form, you are asked to list the important symbols that appear in your dream; you are also to consider how the symbols are related to you.

The symbols are sometimes more disguised than the clearly visible spiral I have already discussed. I recall a dream in which I saw a large spaceship. It was round, disk-shaped, metallic, just like the spaceships in the movies. I see a large door open, and I walk toward it to have a look inside. I am interested in what the "beings" inside might look like. I see some "men" take several human prisoners inside. As I approach the spaceship, however, the door is closed, and I am waved off by guards.

We may ask the question here, What symbol appeared in this dream? It is possible to look at the ship from outer space as a symbol. However, there is an even more basic symbol there. The circle present in the circular shape of the ship is itself a powerful, universal symbol. The circle is widely used to connote unity and perfection, wholeness, or the "ultimate state of Oneness."[3] The feeling it gave me, as I studied a personal flaw which had just surfaced in my life at that time, was of some inner growth which was still eluding me. It was present, visible, and possible, but not yet open to me.

The circle appears in many persons' dreams, often in a disguised fashion. I remember a young woman describing her dream in which she was in the forest at night. She could see dark, hooded figures standing in a circle around a campfire. The mystery and drama of dark, hooded figures standing around a fire in the middle of the forest could easily obscure the basic symbol in this dream—the circle. Thus we sometimes need to look twice for the symbols behind the more obvious images.

The life context and the dream context both influence how we regard a particular symbol. To illustrate, let me tell you of another snake dream much different from the dream discussed earlier.

I have been given a small, green snake to care for. I arrive at a car with several members of my family. A friend helps me tie the snake into a cloth, and I then tie it on the top of the car. We reach the house, and I am concerned about finding some fresh meat for the snake. It seems to need red meat occasionally. I am

making friends with the snake by now. My friend loses
track of it in the garden and cannot find it. But I know
it will turn up as we look for it.

This snake has an entirely different demeanor from the
pursuing, "lashing-out" snake of the other dream. The situation reminded me of a numinous boyhood experience on the
farm where I grew up (a numinous moment being one in
which there is a breaking through into a consciousness of the
world of the spirit). I was about ten years old, and I was
standing roughly ten feet from the creek that ran through
our property. Suddenly a small green snake came wriggling
up the bank from the creek, wrapped itself once around my
ankle and went on its way. I stood breathless, frozen in my
tracks. Then I ran for home.

The snake did not threaten me nor harm me. Yet it was
electrifying. Now, some forty years later, the memory of
that snake is still very much alive in me. And it shows up
again in a dream in which I am to feed and take care of the
snake. As a wise Jungian friend of mine said, "Oh, the
green snake is life energy." The dream came at a time
when I was healing psychically from a painful experience,
and it suggested that my life energy, if fed well, would grow
strong again.

Pay attention to the symbols in your dreams—how they
appear, how they relate to your life, and what they seem to
be saying to you.

Behind the Symbols: Archetypes

According to Dr. Jung, behind every symbol is an archetype
—a basic, hidden psychic pattern in the unconscious, a
center of psychic energy that affects our life deeply. We
never encounter an archetype directly, only through a symbolic representation. For those unfamiliar with Jung's
thought, I will offer one illustration of the archetype.

The hero is one of the important patterns found deep in
the unconscious. We all carry the hero archetype within us,

though what we do with it differs greatly from person to person. Many of us project that hero energy out into the world and look for someone to carry the projection for us— to be hero in our behalf. So we search for someone to be the hero or heroine in our life—a political figure, a ball player, a statesman, a soldier. Or we may use that hero energy to be the hero for ourselves and make our lives what we want them to be. Many let their lives stagnate as they wait for someone on a white horse to come along and make everything right for them.

I once counseled a woman who had never known her father. Her mother had also not known the father, nor did she want to know him. He had come and gone like a thief in the night. At the age of forty-five, my client told me, she was still waiting for the day when her father would come and take her away to a ranch and they would live happily ever after. She had her father and hero archetypes welded together and was waiting for the hero-father to come and make sense of her unhappy life.

The hero archetype (*hero* is not a masculine word here) is very strong in the unconscious, and our society spends millions of dollars every day to seek our heroic figures, male and female, in movies, plays, concerts, and on television. Yet we can often find a strong presence of those archetypal patterns in our dreams.

I recall a startling dream I had several years ago.

I walked into a room and saw a very large brown spider sitting still on the floor. It was possibly eighteen inches across. Feeling frightened, I nevertheless went to find a broom to kill the spider. As I returned to the room where I had seen the huge creature, there was no spider, but a woman was there in its place.

The Jungian analyst with whom I was working at the time, Dr. John Talley of Santa Fe, reminded me of the powerful Indian legends about Spider Woman. Both positive and negative stories are told about her in American Indian lore. In one tradition, Spider Woman is a sort of bogey woman. She sits on her rooftop weaving, only to swoop down on children who have lied to their parents or misbehaved. She then eats them alive, and piles of their bones strew her roof. This is the devouring mother archetype—the scary aspect of every mother that children fear. In fact, grownups fear her just as much. In other stories, Spider Woman is a positive, helpful figure who aids the young hero-warriors in their soul quest.

Thus I needed to explore more deeply and wait for further dream guidance to understand why this feminine archetype was manifesting itself in my dreams. I had to ask questions such as:

- What is this "spider-woman" trying to say to me?
- What is it about my relationship to the inner feminine archetype that I must now confront? What lesson to learn?

One of the fascinating aspects of this relationship to the spider image was how it manifested itself in my outer life in the succeeding months. I would open my car door and find spiders dropping down into my face on their webs as I began to step out of my car. I would find a spider unexplainably dropping from the bare ceiling above me as I sat in my easy chair reading at night. Spiders would show up in my bathroom in unusual numbers. On one occasion, as I discussed a spider dream with Dr. Talley in his office, an ominous-looking spider crawled up out of the chair in which I sat, amazing us both.

When an inner issue intersects with an outer experience in this way, it is called *synchronicity*. This word is from Jung's thought, and it is an important one for our time as we struggle to understand the relationship between our conscious selves and our unconscious.

When an inner event and an outer event happen in conjunction, such as the spider appearing while we discussed spider dreams, we sometimes call it coincidence. But when the conjunction dramatically violates the law of averages and gives us a start or a cold chill, then we must think of it as synchronicity. And we must ask, What is the universe or my inner self trying to tell me? What is the meaning of this strange conjunction of events?

Dream experts often speak of archetypal dreams or "big dreams" as having special energy that may scare or shake us. They often are the dreams that wake us up in the night. I remember one such dream I had in the mountains one night.

I am standing in a clearing in the forest. I raise my arms to the sky and call out, "O Thoth." Something grabs me by the left wrist and jerks me backward, out of control. I am flung out into space and can see stars streaming past me.

I awoke from that dream very frightened and calling, "Help!" At that time I had no knowledge of the name Thoth. I tried to look it up, spelling it Toth, and found nothing. About a month later, because I was still asking, someone told me he had discovered that Thoth, spelled with an "h," was an ancient Egyptian god, the god of wisdom, the ancient Egyptian equivalent of the Greek Hermes (or Mercury), messenger of the gods. It seemed that something very old and deep within me, something archetypal, was grabbing me, trying to get my attention for something important. And indeed it was. Six years later, I am still living out the implications of that dream and that "grabbing."

Archetypal dreams come with great energy, surprising us, scaring us, shaking our foundations. And even though we know we are dealing with great mystery, we must ask (as the dream-journal form points out) about what archetypes are present in our dreams.

If you are not well read in psychology and find archetypes puzzling, simply deal with the questions up to this point and omit the consideration of archetypes.

The Importance of Feelings

The dream-journal form also asks us to consider the feelings we had during or after the dream. The feelings we experience during a dream can be terribly important. Here is a dream in which that was the case:

> *I suddenly remember that I had told someone that I would feed their gerbils in a room at the end of the hall, and I have forgotten all about them. I run down the hall fearing I will find them all dead, as it has been many days since I last fed them. As I approach the door, I see a large, ragged hole in the carpet where one of them has burrowed its way out. I stand looking at the hole and wondering where it might have gone when I feel it attack me from behind. Its teeth are sinking into my shoulder blade. I awaken afraid.*

Several important feelings stand out here. First, there is the awareness that I have neglected an important, instinctual part of myself—kept it locked up and forgotten. This sounds like a dream-image parallel to the psychological mechanism of repression. We push something into the unconscious because the memory is too painful, disturbing, or unacceptable. I also remember feeling guilty as I hurried down the hall. I knew I had neglected something I should have cared for, and that the consequences might be costly. When one of the animals actually attacked me from behind, I felt fear.

If we look at this dream simply through the eyes of feelings, then I, the dreamer, must wonder what I have neglected or failed to give space to in my life. What instinctual part of me has not been fed, and why should I fear its attacking me now?

Some years ago I was leading a workshop in a Colorado town. We began with supper on Friday evening. Next morning at breakfast, one woman approached me and said she had experienced the most horrible dream. She dreamed that she had buried (alive) Jack, one of the men in the workshop. I asked what he represented to her. But she did not know, since she had just met him the night before. When I asked what she was feeling during the burial, she looked embarrassed. "Why, it felt good. Isn't that awful?"

That changed everything. I suggested that perhaps Jack represented some part of her that she needed to bury now. I proposed that she keep an eye on him during the workshop to see what he might symbolize for her. The last morning of the workshop, Jack told his story to the group and began by saying, "I'm a misfit." When the dreamer heard that, she realized that it was the misfit part of her, the tomboy part which had been trying to please her father for 40 years, that she was now ready to bury.

At times we confuse the post-dream feelings with the feelings experienced during the dream. We feel embarrassed the next day as we reflect on some of the things we said or did during the dream. Or we sense that the dream feelings were socially improper and attempt to cancel them out. But the feelings both during and after the dream are important, and both should be added to the dream journal.

The final question on the dream-journal form can be a useful part of your dreamwork; it asks you to consider any other thoughts, ideas, or memories that the dream has triggered in you.

A school teacher once told me a dream in which one of her pupils was a prominent figure. For nearly thirty minutes, we tortured that poor dream with all of the questions we've discussed in this book, plus some I invented on the spot, but we seemed to get nowhere. Finally, exhausted, sweat dripping from my brow, I proposed that we shelve it and work on another dream.

As we gave up the hunt, she suddenly remembered an incident involving the pupil who had appeared in the dream, and she told it to me as an afterthought. The little girl had once come to this teacher at an after-school party and clung to her skirts, crying. Her mother had just arrived to take her home, and she didn't want to leave the party. Now we could understand the dream. The dreamer's mother was due to arrive for a visit the next week, and she felt she would need to conceal signs of her boyfriend's occasional presence in her apartment. The party was over, and she had feelings about it!

On occasion, the idea or memory that the dream triggers is the main task of the dream. Interpretations don't help much until the dreamer devotes some time and energy to reflections on the dream in order to see what else may surface.

Notes
1. J. E. Cirlot, *A Dictionary of Symbols* (London: Routledge & Kegan Paul, 1971), p. 305.
2. Ibid., p. 306.
3. Ibid., pp. 46-47.

6

TURNING YOUR DREAMS UPSIDE DOWN

I remember a young woman who came to a dream class I offered a few years ago. After several sessions, she asked me, "What does it mean if you have dreams of knives and blood all the time?" She looked quite annoyed just mentioning such things. I looked at her sweet, innocent face and observed her posture and gestures. "You are a very nice lady, aren't you?" I asked. "I try to be," she replied. "That's the problem," I told her.

This woman's dream illustrates the important principle of compensation in dreams. She was so "nice" in her outer life that her unconscious compensated or balanced out her imbalance by showing her the opposite—knives and blood. When we are too far out of balance in consciousness, we see the opposite in the unconscious. In other words, this young woman suppressed all her ugly and angry thoughts to be nice, and they gathered in the unconscious as murderous rage.

As Carl Jung once commented, "The unconscious does not harbour in itself any explosive materials unless an overweening or cowardly conscious attitude has secretly laid up stores of explosives there. All the more reason, then, for watching our step."[1]

Behind this dream principle is the assumption that the human unconscious compensates for consciousness, balances out our imbalances, and helps us maintain psychic equilibrium. That means that some dreams can be understood only by turning them upside down and looking at them as though they mean the opposite of what they seem to be saying.

Let us listen to Jung's thoughts on this theme:

> From all this it should now be clear why I make it an heuristic rule, in interpreting a dream, to ask myself: What conscious attitude does it compensate? By so doing, I relate the dream as closely as possible to the conscious situation; indeed, I would even assert that without knowledge of the conscious situation the dream can never be interpreted with any degree of certainty. Only in the light of this knowledge is it possible to make out whether the unconscious content carries a plus or a minus sign. The dream is not an isolated event completely cut off from daily life and lacking its character. If it seems so to us, that is only the result of our lack of understanding, a subjective illusion. In reality the relation between the conscious mind and the dream is strictly causal, and they interact in the subtlest of ways.[2]

At times a dream seems to be portraying a straightforward situation. At other times it seems to be showing us the opposite of what we believe to be the case—a minus sign instead of a plus. A valuable test is to examine the dream in both ways and see which one makes more sense.

Illustrating his point about compensation, Jung tells of a young man who dreamed that his father was driving a new car. The father seems to be driving crazily, and ends by crashing into a wall. The son shouts at him that he should behave himself. The father just laughs, and the son can now see that his father is very drunk.

In reality, the father would never have behaved like that. He is a careful driver and drinks very little. The son and father have a positive relationship. So what does the dream mean? Why does the dream show us such an improbable scene? The truth was that the son's relationship with his father was "too good." He lived too much in the shadow of his father. He was a "daddy's boy" and needed to become more independent, more separate. As Jung then points out, one must know the story of the relationship between this father and son in order to correctly interpret this dream.

Dethroning and Upgrading

Mary Ann Mattoon has spoken of the tendency of dreams "to correct a one-sided attitude in the conscious mind."[3] So we may expect our dreams to dethrone persons, including parents, whom we have put on a pedestal. The dream will usually find a way to depict that "superhuman" person in an uncomplimentary position—which keeps the person human. As Dr. Mattoon explains, "The dream takes a view that is generally opposite to consciousness when the conscious attitude is inadequate or even wrong, or when it threatens the dreamer's perceived needs." She cites the illustration from one of Jung's dreams in which he saw one of his female patients standing high on a castle tower. To see her, he had to bend his head back so far that he got a crick in his neck. When he was honest with himself, he had to admit that he had been looking down on this young woman because of her sexual history, and thus had not been clearly interpreting her dreams. When he admitted this to her and told her the dream, the treatment improved greatly.[4]

I have recently been working with one of my own dreams that I would like to share with you—one that has features of compensation in it.

I am a member of a musical group. We are playing together for the first time—a dance for some singles group. I am to play the piano. We take a lot of time rigging up microphones and electronic equipment. I am worried that I can't play, but the others assure me that I can and not to worry.

Finally we begin. Some people begin dancing. A friend of mine is at the other piano thirty feet away, and he is the lead piano. I provide a second theme or back-up. My piano has some old documents of some kind tucked into it. The music we play is very old tunes which the dancers never heard of. We seem unsure what to play.

This dream felt like a compensatory dream to me, and I will pass on to you some of the work I did with it. First, I am not a musician. I cannot play the piano, and I have not had musical training. When I sang in the junior choir at my church as a boy, the director would stop us and try to locate the one who was off key. So when a dream pictures me playing the piano in a public performance, flags go up. Wait a minute! How is this possible?

If I look at this dream as compensatory, then we may make several assumptions. The dream may be telling me (as the members of the musical group do) that I have hidden musical talent that I have neglected. I'm sure that could be so, for my own tightness as a young person suppressed the music in my soul, and I may need to attend more to music now in my mature years. I should listen to music more often, attend more concerts, try to play some simple instrument. In the language of compensation, then, the absence of music in my conscious life is balanced by my unconscious showing me as a musician. I accept that as a legitimate lesson of this dream.

But there is more: There is one mystery here as well. For one thing, we are playing very old, perhaps ancient, music. There are also these mysterious old documents that seem out of place. To learn more, I sat quietly in a meditative state and went back into the dream—the practice Jungians call active imagination.

I saw myself seated at my piano, as in the dream. (Both pianos in the dream were grand pianos, by the way.) I leaned forward and asked the other piano player why we were playing such old music. "Because," he replied, "this ancient music can awaken old soul memories in you." "Oh," I answered, not knowing much more than I had before. He went on: "The reason these dancers cannot dance to it is because so many modern people are not attuned to listen to the deeper music of their souls. They are listening to the wrong music, living by the beat of a more materialistic sound." That made sense.

There was still the matter of the documents tucked in the piano. I sensed that they were in the piano bench underneath me. I said to my partner, "Could we take a break for a few minutes? I need to check on these old documents." "Sure," he replied.

I saw myself opening the lid on the piano bench. Inside were very old manuscripts. They reminded me of scrolls I had seen in the libraries of the ancient monasteries on northern Greece's Mt. Athos peninsula. In those holy places (where no woman has ever been allowed), I saw manuscripts from as early as the sixth century carelessly piled in bins.

I looked at several of the scrolls in my hands. I couldn't seem to understand them, so I scooped them up and took them with me to the place of my Inner Teacher. This interior psychic presence is a deep reality to me. It is a guardian angel or spirit guide with whom I discuss my dreams. I walked into his room and put the scrolls down on his table. He asked, "What do you have there?" I answered that they were ancient documents from my dream, and that I needed help in understanding them. My teacher picked one up and looked at it with me. "They are in Sanskrit," he told me, "the ancient holy language of the people of India." My ears perked up, for I was soon to lead a tour of holy places in India and Nepal. "There is a relationship between these sacred documents and music. In India, you will be hearing music, and music to the Hindu is sacred sound. It is not separate from the holy, as you Westerners have made it. Indeed, you need to attune your soul to music in preparation for your pilgrimage to India and Nepal." I had heard enough. What had seemed a simple compensatory dream about the neglect of music in my life had turned out to be much more. It was much deeper, much more profound than I had imagined. And so I am currently turning to music in an effort to open my soul to God in a deeper way.

The Issue of Control

Here is a much simpler compensatory dream that appears in various forms quite often in my dreaming.

I am leading a workshop for a small group in a home somewhere. Members of the group begin leaving the room, coming in and out so that it is difficult to continue. Some are baking cakes. The work I am trying to do with them falls apart.

In my understanding of this dream, the situation raises the issue of control. When I lead a workshop, I like a "tight ship." I do not like people coming and going, as it disturbs the flow of energy in the group, breaking up the interaction. I prefer that people arrive on time at the beginning of the workshop and stay through to the finish. There is value in that; much more can be accomplished when the group energy builds and is held intact. However, the dream is raising this issue for review, so what is it trying to tell me?

If my dream depicts me losing control, what is that compensating in consciousness? That seems to be the right question to ask. I must consider the possibility that I lean toward too much control, which is compensated in the dream by a loss of control. Perhaps I am a bit too rigid in this respect. However, my over-control does not really appear in my leadership of workshops. I do a good job there and have never had complaints about that. Perhaps, then, my over-control appears in another area of my life! Perhaps I over-control in my therapy sessions; I will look at that possibility. More likely, however, is the chance that I am over-controlling in my relationships with my children. I must take a closer look at how I exercise authority and leadership with my children, and with my sons in particular. This interpretation feels right to me.

Where does this compensation factor originate? If dreams try to balance what is out of balance in our conscious life, what is the source of that balancing effort? And why do dreams work that way? According to Jung, there is a movement toward wholeness in the human psyche. This inherent process, which Jung calls the process of individuation, is incredibly important. It works in the unconscious all the time, moving us toward a wholeness of life and spirit, guiding us to become the persons we are really meant to be. In the process we are sometimes led into more pain, not away from it.

It is painful to confront ourselves, see who we really are, accept our shadow side, and give up the foolish masks we put on to hide our reality from others. So the compensatory function in dreams works toward balancing the accounts and showing us what is out of kilter; it invites us to make the necessary changes to move on in our growth. And of course we can always ignore these lessons. We can admit, see, and accept what the unconscious is showing us but continue on as before, refusing to take the necessary steps, the inevitable risks, to change our lives. However, when we neglect the inner leadings toward wholeness, we do so at real peril to our own growth.

Notes
1. C. G. Jung, *Dreams* (Princeton, N.J.: Princeton University Press, 1974), p. 102.
2. Ibid.
3. Mary Ann Mattoon, *Applied Dream Analysis: A Jungian Approach* (Washington, D.C.: V. H. Winston & Sons, 1978), p. 120.
4. Ibid., p. 124.

7

PURSUING THE DREAM

While spending a semester at the C. G. Jung Institute in
Zurich in 1973, I began my own dream analysis in earnest.
My analyst was a wise English woman named Andrea
Dykes. One day I discussed a simple dream with her:

> *A glacier has somehow appeared in the valley near
> Zurich, though glaciers belong many miles away in
> the high mountains. I am tempted to go see the glacier,
> but I note how the streets are jammed with traffic as
> people in cars, trucks, motorcycles, and bicycles are
> rushing out to see this strange sight. I decide I will go
> later, when it isn't so crowded.*

Miss Dykes did not say much about the dream. She
implied that I had missed the point and that I needed to go
back to my glacier to see what it meant. *(Rule of thumb for
dreamwork: When something is grossly out of place, pay
special attention!)* She suggested using a meditative method
Jung called active imagination to return to the dream.

Active imagination has been known by many other names
in other cultures and therapy systems. It is a powerful tool
for insight, personal growth, and personality transformation. Jung did not write a great deal about it, though he used
the method with his patients and for his own inner exploration. He feared the average person was not yet ready for it.
Persons with a weak ego structure, who typically are not
clear about their readiness to explore the unconscious,
should not attempt active imagination. However, I believe
that we as a people are much stronger than we were 50 years
ago: We are more ready to explore our inner being, and we

bring more ego strength to the task. As a result, far more is being written and spoken about active imagination today.

One way to describe active imagination is to see it as a process in which we sit on the boundary between consciousness and the unconscious in order to mediate a conversation between the two. The unconscious "speaks," usually in the form of images; it is much like watching a color movie in which we are also participants. Some persons do not see images but perceive in a different way, through the senses. They will not report what they "see" but what they feel or sense is happening. That is still valid active imagination and can reveal deep truths to us. I usually see visual images when I practice active imagination.

A few days after my challenge from Andrea Dykes, I was prepared to explore the glacier of my dream. I set aside some time when I would be alone. Next I sat quietly in my room with both feet on the floor, closed my eyes, and purposely drew my awareness in with my breath.

As I closed my eyes and followed my breath inside, I was aware that it is important not to daydream or think up an answer or picture. Waiting on the unconscious is the goal of active imagination, and we must learn to be patient. I suddenly saw the glacier, but it had melted a great deal; I was faced with a surprise. Whenever our images surprise us, we can usually be sure we have not "made them up," that they are genuine offerings of the inner self.

My glacier had melted back to reveal an old pirate ship with rotten, tattered sails hanging from the masts. I could see some pirates running around the ship fixing things up after its long period of disrepair. There was a ladder that led right up to the deck, so I climbed aboard. I felt a bit awed by this whole experience and sensed that something important was happening.

As I climbed aboard, an old pirate menacingly approached me and asked what I was doing there. (He didn't realize it was *my* ship and *my* glacier.) I told him I wanted to talk with his "leader." I was led to the pirate chief, who really looked like a classic pirate. He had no shirt on and wore a long knife or sword in his belt. He looked me over suspiciously, but as we began to talk, I found I liked him. Soon we were laughing and enjoying each other's company. He brought out a table, and we sat down for some wine, cheese, and fruit.

All of a sudden, the pirate chief said to me, "If they find out what we've got in that hold back there, your name will be mud." *(Rule of thumb for dreamwork: When things happen suddenly in a dream, pay special attention!)* I looked at him in shock and asked what his hold could possibly have to do with me (forgetting that it was my ship). He took me to the stern of the ship and showed me a big hatch on the deck secured by a large rusty padlock.

I decided that I needed to open the hatch and see what was there that would reflect on me if discovered. I found a crowbar and broke the lock open. I peered down into the darkness below, where I could hear moaning and the clanking of chains. A terrible stench came up from the hold. I found a ladder and climbed below. I could tell there were people shackled down there, and I felt I should release them. I knocked out some of the boarded-up windows (or portholes) and let some light into the darkness. I found a hose and began washing down the filthy floor. Then I began releasing the prisoners one at a time. The first one to be released was my father, and he went directly to the ladder and climbed out. (My father had been dead for many years at the time of this dream, but I found I had emotional business with him that was not finished.) Each person shackled in that terrible hold was a person with whom I had unfinished or unresolved personal business. When I had done all I could, I noticed that a large shadowy area remained back at the end of the ship, which was still frozen into the unmelted portion of the glacier.

Frozenness

Frozenness usually implies that we have repressed areas of our personality—have shut off feelings and memories that are best released. The active imagination I had experienced was very vivid, and it is still alive and active in my psyche. I continue to learn from it each time I share it with an audience or ponder its meaning more deeply. Let me share some of the reflections and insights produced by this powerful stream of images and actions.

First, there is a pirate part of me that feels he can take whatever he wants or needs without asking. This is probably not a large part of me, but one that I must stay conscious of. (There is a pirate part of everyone, an archetypal presence that can influence our daily lives.)

Perhaps more important, this active imagination showed me a classic image of my shadow side. Below the decks, in the unconscious, are many unresolved issues from my past, shadow elements of my life that take energy to repress and keep hidden. My task, if I want to grow into wholeness, is to keep bringing those hidden secrets into the light so I can examine them, learn from them, and release them from my inner prison.

Recently I learned one more fascinating truth from this active imagination. A friend reminded me that one of the dangers of locking people below decks is that they might one day mutiny and take over the ship. Naturally it's far better to work on letting them go before they revolt and take over. While opening the hold of our inner being may seem disgusting, the net result is a feeling of lightness and clearness with ourself.

One further note about active imagination: I was dealing with an image from my unconscious, but I was there with the full strength of my conscious ego self. I was an active participant in the process, not an observer. This experience is different from a passive fantasy that we merely observe. I made decisions about how to approach the pirate chief and whether or not I was ready to open the hold. My ego was active and contributing to the process. Marie-Louise von Franz refers to this as "the active, ethical confrontation, the active entering of the whole person into the fantasy-drama."[1] Dr. von Franz, a leading Jungian analyst and scholar, calls active imagination "the most powerful tool in Jungian psychology for achieving wholeness—far more efficient than dream interpretation alone." She adds, " . . . nobody who has once discovered active imagination would ever want to miss it, because it can literally achieve miracles of inner transformation."[2]

Surely the best writing on active imagination is Barbara Hannah's *Encounters with the Soul: Active Imagination.* Jungian analyst Hannah says, "Perhaps the simplest definition of active imagination is to say that it gives us the opportunity of opening negotiations, and in time, coming to terms, with these forces or figures in the unconscious. In this aspect, it differs from the dream, for we have no control over our own behavior in the latter."[3]

Ned's Dream

One man in his mid-forties (let's call him Ned) came to me for therapy—therapy that later included the use of active imagination. I asked Ned to write down any dreams he remembered and bring them to the next session. He reported one dream as follows:

> *I am walking along a river bank, looking down into the water as I walk. I notice something in the water at the bottom of the river. It looks like a dark box, shaped like a coffin, and it has a bright red star on it.*

At this point, I had to make an assessment. We could have discussed what red stars mean, even what the symbol of the star has meant historically. Instead, having decided that Ned had plenty of ego strength, I asked him to close his eyes. I suggested that he take some deep breaths and sit with his back straight. I watched as his body relaxed with the breathing; then I said, "Now go back to the river bank, and tell me when you are there." After a few moments, Ned nodded and said, "Yes, I can see the coffin down there with the red star on it." I asked if he was willing to open the coffin and see what was in it, and he said he was. I suggested several options for Ned to think about. "You could put on a diver's suit and go down to the bottom of the river to see if you can open the coffin there. Or you could get a crane and have it hoisted up from the bottom." "It's already up," he reported. "It's sitting on the river bank."

I asked Ned if he could open the coffin and see what was in it. Next I explained that it could be very important for him to dredge up this buried part of his unconscious and see what it had to say to him. He replied, "It's already open. I know who's in there; it's my mother!" I could see the fear and hesitation in his face, and I asked him what he was afraid of. "I'm afraid of what she may say to me," he answered. As it turned out, he was also afraid of his own anger toward his mother. Through further therapy, he worked on the difficult emotional relationship with his mother, raised to the surface by the dream and the active imagination that followed it.

Ned was a prime candidate for using active imagination. He picked it up on his first try, and it has been an invaluable tool for him ever since. Jungian experts often speak of holding back with active imagination until a client has been in analysis for some time. I tend to introduce it much sooner— *if* the client has enough ego strength, in my estimation, to provide a firm platform from which to explore the unconscious. Some people have great difficulty getting into active imagination or seem completely unable to do so. Yet I am often amazed at how many can pick it up easily and use it as a natural tool. Perhaps our evolution makes us increasingly ready to reclaim the unconscious and the body as part of our wholeness.

There are several reasons why I believe, as a therapist, that it is helpful to use active imagination in my office with my clients, rather than relying on them to do it alone at home. I feel my presence gives people the confidence to trust what they are seeing or perceiving when they do active imagination with an image. I sometimes coach clients to trust their ability to confront the image and learn from it. "Ask what it is trying to say to you," I may suggest. "Why has it come into your dream?" I do not interfere in the process of the interaction, but I do offer suggestions to encourage the person to learn from the unconscious image and to trust that it can reply.

Very often clients trying active imagination will report that they saw something or heard something, "but I don't know if I just made it up." I encourage them to take it seriously rather than dismissing it as an invention of their mind. After the fact, it is important to test the information with the mind. Historically, we have exalted our thinking function and downgraded our intuitive processes as unreliable and untrustworthy. Active imagination reverses that process. It is essential that we reclaim intuition and its incredible gifts, but we don't have to throw out the mind to do so. We need to use the mind to test the reasonableness of what we learn from intuitive processes such as active imagination. Then we can decide what action we should take to translate our decisions into daily life.

Trusting the Images

A friend of mine once nearly dismissed a powerful image that was very important for him. Nearly all his life, he had put himself down, saying that he was a terrible person. When I would ask Charles why he felt that way, he would reply that he had always known it and people had always told him that. I asked him to close his eyes, take some deep breaths, and get relaxed. I said, "Now ask your unconscious to take you back to the time when you decided you are a terrible person, and tell me what you see."

After a few moments, Charles opened his eyes and said, "Oh, that's crazy! That couldn't have anything to do with this." I asked him to let me help decide if something was crazy. "What did you actually see?" "I saw the afterbirth," he replied. (The afterbirth is the tissue material that protects and nourishes a child in the womb.) I asked him to close his eyes once again and go back inside to see the scene again. "I see the afterbirth again," he said, "and it's yucky." As Charles had used the same word to describe himself many times, I knew we had hit on an important piece of history. As we discussed it, Charles revealed that he apparently made a decision at birth that *he* was yucky. He may have heard someone say that word in the delivery room, and his unconscious, inner being heard it as applied to him. He somehow identified with the afterbirth and felt he was yucky, no good, unlovable. When he began to realize this connection he had made, he felt better about himself.

Traditional psychology has not allowed the possibility that infants in the womb or newborns can record impressions and make decisions that affect their entire lives. Many of us who work with the unconscious feel differently. We frequently hear material that can have come only from the prenatal period and from an aware, conscious being (even though regarded by adults as unable to hear or understand). The psychological process called rebirthing takes us back into the womb to reexperience those critical moments and see how they have affected us as adults. Many psychologists now acknowledge these mysterious realms and their role in revealing secrets that conventional therapy does not usually touch. Active imagination is the powerful tool available to us for reentry into the unconscious. It is especially *active* imagination when we take an active part in the imaged material. Charles made it active imagination by going back to that moment of birth to reconsider his understanding of the afterbirth.

Dreams as Invitation

I want to propose one theory that I have not found in other discussions of dreams. I believe that many dreams cannot be interpreted, no matter how expert the interpreter or analyst, because they are not intended to be interpreted! Many dreams do not lend themselves to interpretation because they are no more than invitations to dialogue with the unconscious. They prod, provoke, tantalize, rattle our cage, even shake us up so we will turn our attention inward and listen.

If this is true, then we must learn to distinguish between dreams that ask for interpretation and dreams that are merely invitations to turn inward. When symbolism is clearly present, when persons are identifiable, when feelings are prominent, then perhaps interpretation is the place to begin. When none of these obvious handles is available, then we may be justified in regarding the dream as invitation. *Active imagination is the tool with which we respond to the dream's invitation.* It is the method we must use to explore the dream more deeply, to ask the dream what it is trying to say to us. Active imagination opens the door for something else to happen, for insight, wisdom, guidance to enter our awareness. Invitation dreams are very important, but dream literature has largely ignored them because it did not have the tool of active imagination to crack open the invitational dream. We now have that tool—*if* we are strong enough to use it and *if* we are willing to risk learning how to use it.

I believe my glacier dream was an invitation to explore my own shadow. Interpreting the meaning of an out-of-place glacier simply would not have allowed the rich personal material revealed by my active imagination to unfold. I believe Ned's dream of the coffin at the bottom of the river was also an invitation. Let me offer another illustration of a dream that I understand as an invitation to deeper exploration.

Jean, a young woman, had the following dream:

> *I see a young boy-child dying. He is about a year and a half or two years old. My therapist is holding a Saturday group session, and I don't want to go, but I do.*

The first question this dream raises is what the boy-child's dying represents. Looking up *child* or *death* in a dream dictionary would not give the personal context in which to explain such a dream. I suggested to Jean that she close her eyes and talk to the child in the dream. She was experienced in active imagination, so she did not hesitate. She sat with her back straight, took a few deep breaths, and became quietly relaxed. I said softly, "Talk to him out loud. Do you see him yet?" "Yes," she replied.

"What do you have to tell me?" she asked. "What part of me are you?" The answer: "I am the needy, emotional part of you, and I don't want to die. You have been neglecting me and failing to nourish me. You need to tear down that wall you have built up around me and let people into your life. You are emotionally starving yourself."

Jean agreed, with tears in her eyes, that she had been "toughing it out" lately and had not allowed herself to be weak and needy. She needed to allow some time for tears so that her strength could return. Many of us, like Jean, present a strong front to the world and try to ignore our emotional side. Our feelings may then gang up on us and erupt in some unpleasant way. Jean had to make the choice about how she would handle her new awareness. She could choose to continue burying her feelings, or she could tear down her wall and allow the needy child some time and space in her life.

I have had clients who agreed to paint or sketch their dreams. This is an excellent way to objectify the dream, to place it in front of us in a concrete way. Aspects of truth often emerge in the shapes, colors, and patterns of paintings and sketches that do not appear in a dream's verbal description. I urge you to attempt drawing and painting your dream images. You don't need to be an artist. Simply do the painting for yourself.

Once the painting has been studied, I often invite my client to enter into the painting with active imagination. This can further and deepen the work of the unconscious begun by the dream, developed by the painting, and continued by the active work of reentering the scene in imagination. This is dreamwork at its best.

Another form of active imagination that can be very powerful is to dance the dream (or a scene from it). Anyone can express feelings and actions in movement without being a professional dancer.

Dr. Edith Wallace has stressed that active imagination sometimes replaces dreaming: A person who listens intently to the unconscious through active imagination may find fewer dreams visiting his or her sleep.

The Spiritual Realm

Both dreams and active imagination often touch the deep, spiritual realm of our being. Here are two illustrations of this powerful role that dreams can play in our lives.

Marcia was a nun, struggling with issues of her identity and her commitment to the religious life and to celibacy. She presented a dream one day that she entitled "Divine Visitation."

> *I am at home sleeping. My sister is also there. It is just before dawn. A surgeon appears and kisses my lips and asks if I will make love with him. I feel violated.*

Marcia's comment on the dream was that "he seemed like Christ, the divine surgeon." From a Jungian perspective, we would immediately suspect that this unknown person of opposite sex was Marcia's *animus,* her masculine self inviting her to deeper connection and union with him. And indeed that could be so. But I suspected there was something else here. The dream had spiritual overtones, referred to by Marcia, that seemed to point beyond the animus interpretation. I suggested she do an active imagination with the surgeon figure and see what else she could learn.

As Marcia closed her eyes and pulled her awareness inside herself, she reported that she could see the surgeon of her dream. "I have a sense that he is death and that this was the kiss of death," she said. I proposed that she ask him about this. "Why did you kiss me?" she asked. The surgeon replied that it was not intimacy he was seeking. "I want you to follow me," he said.

"You want me to follow you? I'm not comfortable with you; you're too masked." He takes off his mask and reveals himself as blonde, youngish, and bearded. "Who are you?"

Marcia asks him. "You remind me of a young man I once knew." Then she tells me, "I sense that he is a divine messenger. This is an invitation to enter more deeply into the inner part of myself—to engage the real self."

At moments like this, I always feel deeply moved and honored to be sharing the sacred moments (the *numinous* moments) of a person's soul. Such moments are not uncommon when we work deeply with the unconscious. Marcia moved toward the end of her two years of therapy at her next session, and I do not believe it was accidental that her invitation to a deeper connection with the inner self came when it did.

Another dream has similar qualities—again from a single woman in mid-life, Portia.

I am in a vast cathedral, as in Europe. A novice-mistress (the most unlikely person in the world) announces she is getting married. She has deliberated and planned this marriage a long time. The groom has grayish hair. His clothes are translucent. People at the wedding comment, "My God, they resemble each other." The church is full.

The bride, the former novice-mistress, makes her vows from behind the groom with her hands on his head. She promises "honesty, no phoniness in facing present reality." She speaks of being aware of her family's possible embarrassment at her marriage. He remains silent. The church darkens, and thunder rumbles outside. It is as though God has recognized this event and given his okay.

As the bride passes before me, I tell her, "You are so beautiful." I go through a tunnel into a courtyard. Dark clouds are hanging low.

This dream of a marriage puzzled Portia. She had taken vows as a celibate religious woman many years before and had no intention of marrying. So what was the meaning of a carefully planned marriage in her dream? I suggested that she talk to the bride and groom and see what they had to tell her. They spoke:

> *We are a part of your self. There is now a powerful coming together of things within you at a much deeper level. You are allowing your inner self to join more deliberately with your conscious self. To put it another way, the animus is now recognized at a deeper level as an essential part of your self. You have been preparing for this in a deliberate way. . . .*

The active imagination provided guidance and wisdom from the unconscious to help Portia unlock her dream. She discovered the deep, spiritual union of consciousness and the unconscious, the inner marriage that Jung called the *royal marriage*—the enlargement of the self within to include the ego consciousness and form a more complete person, a truly whole being. This discovery can be a great moment in a person's development.

The goal and purpose of using active imagination with my clients in my office is to encourage them to try it on their own. I invite them to develop their own resources for unlocking their dreams, rather than relying on me or another person to provide answers for them.

I believe that my experience and comfort with active imagination is contagious. Clients who practice it in a session in my office can see how powerful the images and messages are, and they find a validation in my response. When they realize I take their imagination seriously and treat it as truth, they can regard it more seriously themselves. Many of them learn to try active imagination on their own and come to their therapy sessions not only with their dreams to report but also with the results of their own inner explorations of the dreams.

We have just begun to scratch the surface when it comes to unlocking the power of our dreams for making us whole. And we have just begun to learn how to use active imagination as a tool for opening to us the riches and mystery of the unconscious.

Notes
1. Marie-Louise von Franz, introduction to Barbara Hannah, *Encounters with the Soul: Active Imagination* (Santa Monica, Calif.: Sigo Press, 1981), p. 1.
2. Ibid., p. 2.
3. Ibid., p. 16.

8

DREAMS AND THE INNER TEACHER

An exciting new phenomenon is breaking on the horizon. This phenomenon is found in persons exploring their inner frontiers, persons on their spiritual journey. Now is the time of the inner teacher. For many centuries, people have looked for great teachers, leaders, gurus, and champions to show us how to live. We have relied on systems of religious or political thought to show us how to behave and think of ourselves. Millions still need those systems, and they will be important for many years to come. But there is evidence of the coming of a new age.

In the past, only the rare pioneering spirit dared to defy the system in which he or she had grown up in order to follow the leading of the inner voice. Today, that inner leading is becoming the property of more and more people. Increasingly, people are learning to listen to and trust the deep inner wisdom of their souls, even when it differs from popular opinion, parental training, and social upbringing. Historically, religious authorities have feared such inner leading as the work of the devil. Today we are much more ready to trust that God works from deep within us. When we learn to trust the inner teacher, and to check our dreams with that teacher, our lives begin to flow with the divine intention.

In order to use the incredible resource of the inner teacher, first you must believe that there is an inner world that is just as real as the world of ordinary consciousness. Secondly, you must believe that there is personal guidance for your life in that inner world, in the core of your inner

being. Finally, you must be willing to practice the meditative discipline of turning your attention inward to seek the
inner teacher. For many people, this is hard work. We are
such activists that we want things to happen easily and
quickly. Active imagination requires patience and the will-
ingness to practice and devote time to the endeavor.

Two additional points are important in this process. Once
we have found our inner teacher, we must trust the teacher's
guidance, just as we must learn to trust our intuition and our
active imagination. Finally, we need to put into action what
we have heard and believed.

The story of Dr. Brugh Joy is an inspiring example of the
emergence of the inner teacher. Brugh Joy was a distin-
guished physician in Los Angeles prior to 1974. He had
graduated from the University of Southern California
(USC) School of Medicine, interned at Johns Hopkins Hospital, and then gone on to be a resident at the Mayo Clinic in
Rochester, Minnesota. In Los Angeles he was a physician
and an assistant clinical professor of medicine at USC.

In the late 1960s, at the age of twenty-seven, while still at
the Mayo Clinic, Brugh had an intuitive flash that he would
find a female spiritual teacher in Los Angeles with whom he
would study. He felt this would happen within a few years,
while he was in his early thirties. This puzzled him, because
he had no intention at that time of returning to Los Angeles,
because he did not like living there. Two years later, sta-
tioned in San Diego with the Navy, he had an image of the
woman who was to become his teacher, though he still had
no intention of returning to Los Angeles. However, in his
last year of naval service, he was offered an opportunity to
share a partnership with two well-known physicians in Los
Angeles. He accepted.

In the meantime, Brugh's earlier interest in paranormal
experiences and metaphysics, set aside during his medical
studies, was rekindled. He felt a "deep yearning to explore
higher states of consciousness." In 1971, one of his patients
suggested that he might enjoy meeting a spiritual teacher
named Eunice Hurt. When Brugh and Eunice met, there

was instant recognition on both their parts that they were intended to work together. Brugh cried tears of great joy that night, tears of recognition.

Brugh studied with Eunice for only a year before her death from cancer, but the year transformed his life. Her teaching had a profound effect on him. For example, he began setting aside at least an hour each morning to enter a state of deep meditation. At times, this meant getting up at 4 A.M. after long days at the hospital and his office. At the time of Eunice's death, Brugh felt he would find no other teacher to take her place. And indeed this was to be the case. In his words:

> How many times have I observed people sitting in living rooms, lecture halls, or in mountain retreats, listening to an inspired teacher. Some of these people had been doing the same thing for a year, five years, even forty years. After all that time they still persist in failing to realize that the critical step is in being, not in what is spoken about being. Action must be taken, and that action is inside.
>
> Almost two months to the day after Eunice's death, I found my Inner Teacher—a state of consciousness that continues to teach me today. It is not a manifestation of Eunice or of anybody else that I recognize in my outer mind. Its presence is radiant; and its wisdom, inspiring.[1]

I have also found the inner teacher to be inspiring, its guidance profound. My first experience with an inner teacher came as I sat on a beach in Greece several years ago. Brugh's book, *Joy's Way,* had just been published, but I had not yet seen it. I had, however, just completed a two-week cruise with 350 Americans visiting ancient healing centers in the Mediterranean, followed by a one-week retreat on a Greek island. One of the faculty members for this experience had been Dr. Brugh Joy. Another was Rosalyn Bruyere, noted healer and psychic, who has cooperated with much current research on healing energy.

During the island retreat, Rosalyn explained to us that she often receives wisdom and guidance from an inner teacher, a Chinese wise man. Several weeks later, I spent five days on the secluded Mt. Athos peninsula. I stayed in ancient monasteries, some over 1,000 years old, and sampled the life of a medieval monk. As I came away from those five days, I landed in a small fishing village, where I began notes for a book on pilgrimage.

As I sat on the beach one day, deep in meditation, my thoughts turned to Rosalyn Bruyere; I wished I could ask her about several questions in my mind. To my amazement, I felt the presence of the Chinese wise man introduced to us by Rosalyn. Ever since that day on the beach in Greece, I have from time to time consulted that inner teacher about a variety of matters. Invariably, his guidance has been appropriate and helpful.

I have often wondered if I would or should find a teacher with whom to study spiritual matters. I have spent time with many outstanding teachers, but I never felt I was to follow one teacher or guru. About a year ago, I asked a wise old spiritual woman about this. "Am I supposed to find a teacher to follow, and if so, when? And let's get on with it."

The answer was crystal clear. I was not to follow a single teacher or group. Rather, I was to rely on the Christ-spirit within me. The spiritual woman's guidance felt genuine and also fit with my own intuition. I have believed and acted on it ever since. I have ceased looking for one teacher, and now I turn to the inner teacher. I also feel that it is my responsibility to help others find that teacher in themselves.

When I had the opportunity, soon after the guidance from this wise woman, I checked this belief with my own inner guidance. In active imagination, I consulted the Christ within me and asked him if I were now to rely on the inner teacher. In answer, he took me by the hand and led me to a cave in which an old man lived. He was partly bald, short, and a little stooped. His face is always smiling and receptive, though his words for me are not always comfortable. I was told, "This teacher will represent me to you. Come talk with him about anything, and he will answer in my name." I felt a great sense of relief that I was not to follow some guru and a sense of joy at having a teacher to consult on a regular basis. I often discuss my dreams with him, and I take to him the knotty problems of life so that he can help me reflect on what I should do. This does not mean that I refuse to learn from some of the other great teachers of today. I do so quite frequently: I attend lectures; I read books; I talk with outstanding people whenever I can; I go to workshops. But I do not follow any one teacher, taking everything that teacher says as absolute truth.

I am certain that the best dream interpretations come from this wisdom found within us. Such wisdom has always been suspect because it is considered "merely human." When we dismiss inner guidance as "merely human," we downgrade the depth and mystery of the human. We also deny the presence of God's active and living spirit within us. Thus we are splitting God's creation into "God out there" and "merely human." I believe that God acts within us and through us, that the living spirit of God is present in me and in you.

And so when I dream, I am always aware of the possibility that God may speak to me through those dreams, guiding my life, showing me my imbalances and my shortcomings, challenging and inspiring me. I know that God lives in the deep unconscious, wherever else God may preside. This living God within, who also is present throughout the universe and beyond, is incredibly real. When we live in our surface selves, we do not know this living presence within us; therefore we also deny that others could have it.

One of my friends had two dreams within the space of a few days that show the power of the inner teacher and illustrate one of the ways that this teacher can come to us. In her first dream, Amanda walks into a fabric store. A little elf or dwarf tells her to follow him upstairs. People are dancing in the store. There were other details in this dream, but the little person stood out. Amanda decided to do an active imagination with this figure.

When she had gotten quiet and centered, Amanda approached the dwarf person and asked him why he had come and what he wanted to say to her. He replied, "I'm from the underworld, and I'm here to guide and to reassure you when you are going through dark and creepy places." She reported that the little man was "ugly, but cute." He tells her that he has been sent to lead her to her teacher.

In a flash, the scene changed and they were sitting in a clearing in the forest. Amanda then realized that her guide had vanished and a wise old man was sitting next to her. It felt awesome to be next to him. The wise man tells Amanda that she is to spend more time with him from now on. The little person from the dream had been there to lead her to this wise man. "You are embarking on a great spiritual journey," he tells her. "You will have to give up some things very personal to you. There will be a guide to help you who has reverence and understanding for your sensitive spirit." Amanda feels frightened as she hears all this. He tells her she has been preparing for this for a long time. The wise old man figure then changes, and she sees the figure of Jesus. He speaks to her and says, "I am with you always. I have never left you."

This was a very moving moment for both Amanda and me. It was a moment of deep vision, a moment of spiritual calling from the depths of her being. Should she disregard this as nonsense that she had made up in a rush of megalomania? Some psychologists would dismiss it because they hold a narrow definition of sanity. I believe Amanda should test such an experience with her rational mind to see if it makes sense to her and to her situation in life. If it seems reasonable, then she should regard it as absolutely genuine and base her future actions upon it. That is what she chose to do.

A dream she had ten days later was also interesting.

Four or five of us go to visit an old house on a plateau. It is in a wooded area and has a big garden. I see a huge beet above ground but not fully grown. It has huge leaves. In the house someone brings out a large

*oval-shaped mother-of-pearl platter. It has gold inlay
like lace and is awesomely beautiful.*

What was the meaning of this oval-shaped, gold-inlaid
platter? Why did it appear in her dream? For the answer,
Amanda went inside herself to discuss it with the wise old
man who had appeared to her a few days earlier. As the old
man appears, Amanda greets him; then she tells him that
she wants some guidance about the platter. She describes it
to him and says, "I feel excited at how beautiful it is—warm
and glowing." He replies, "Part of you is pure gold—the
part that is his—God's. It is the part that has surrendered in
a loving embrace, the part that is passionately and fiercely
wedded to God. That is a kind of sacred union. It is part of
you you must always treasure, always hold before you. . . .
Know your beauty. The time is now for you to know your
beauty."

Again, this was a deeply moving and numinous moment
for Amanda. It confirmed that she was on the right path in
her spiritual journey, that she had deep confirmation from
her unconscious. The figure of the wise old man will always
be with her, always available for her to consult. The dream
provided the invitation in the form of the dwarf, active imagination provided the tool for exploring it, and the inner
teacher provided the wisdom.

A young friend recently shared the following dream
with me:

*We're at the home where I grew up. My grandfather is
there, but I don't know him. He could be my father's
father who died before I was born. We are walking
down the front walk, and he cuts off slices of apple as
we walk and throws them for me to catch.*

*Then he begins sweating. He takes off some of his
clothes, then staggers and falls. I'm crying, and I lie
across his chest. I tell him, "Don't die now; I love
you." Then I'm in the house and my brother Jim
comes in. He says, "I think Grandfather died." I am
angry that no one had told me, and I won't talk to*

anyone. Somebody tells me I have diabetes. My sister comes in and gives me some little bells from a primitive Filipino necklace.

We discussed this dream for a time, and then I suggested to Ann, the dreamer, that she talk with the grandfather figure in the dream. I told her he seemed important to me and that she needed to know more about why he had appeared in her dream. Ann agreed, closed her eyes, got herself centered by deep breathing, and said she could see the grandfather figure now.

"He's been watching me for a long time," she says. "He tells me I've been going in circles, and he has come to give me a push. I asked him what I should be doing, and he tells me I need to take a different direction. Then I asked him, 'Who are you really?' and he changed. He looks like a wizard! He is someone who knows things without being distracted by the outer garbage the way I am. He says I need somebody there all the time poking me." Then Ann consulted her wizard/grandfather figure about the dream, and he gave her valuable additional insights into its meaning.

Here was a marvelous example of a dream leading Ann to her inner teacher through active imagination. We could also call this wizard figure an image of the wise old man archetype, to use Jungian language. The important thing is that his wisdom and insight will be available to her on a regular basis at a time when Ann is struggling with the boredom in her life. If she chooses to ignore him and continue with her life as it is, he will surely give her another push.

The inner teacher can help with less lofty dreams as well. It is my practice to discuss some of my dreams with my inner teacher. Not long ago, I dreamed:

A young, rebellious officer has challenged the ruling prince to a duel. I am a referee. The prince has an automatic pistol. The rebel has a good pistol and is confident he will hit the prince before the ruler can fire the deadly automatic pistol. I do not trust the prince, and I warn both that if either fires before the count of three, I will kill him myself.

Then, as they stall around, I take the opportunity to suggest that they talk with each other to see if they might work it out and avoid the duel. They decide to do this.

I was unclear about what this dream was trying to tell me, so I consulted my inner teacher the next morning. He told me that there is a rebellious maverick in me who stands in conflict with the hot-headed young ruler part of me. The hot-headed ruler is the arrogant, self-righteous part of me that makes demands and expects things to go his way. My conscious ego must abandon the safe position of neutrality and actively negotiate a resolution of this inner conflict, or it can really hurt me. If they can work out their differences, it will free a lot of wasted energy.

I take this information very seriously. The dream is dealing with what Jung would call "personal shadow material," hidden parts of me that I need to know more deeply. The inner teacher can be very useful in focusing my attention and intellect on the issues raised by the dream. After all, my own inner self knows far better than anyone what I need to confront, what I am capable of absorbing, and how I might proceed with it.

Who Is Ready?

"How can I know if I am supposed to rely on an inner teacher now?" you may ask. "Is it only the spiritual elite who have an inner teacher?"

Your own intuition is the best guide to answer this question. The inner teacher is certainly not the property of a limited number of spiritual leaders, but belongs to all of us. The time is rapidly arriving for the masses of people to turn to this natural, inner guidance for their lives, rather than depending upon collective wisdom handed down by organizations.

When we turn inward to our unconscious for insight, we often find an abundance of images addressing us. Our inner wisdom comes to us in many guises, and we must always test it through the medium of our good sense. That good sense will have been tempered and influenced by the teachings of our parents, our religion, and the dictates of our culture. If our inner leading is too far afield from what we believe to be right and proper, then we must carefully consider dismissing it. If we are uncertain, we certainly should not take action until we feel clear about it.

I would like to digress for a moment to make a historical observation. In the early period of Christianity, a group we refer to as Gnostics were known for honoring their inner guidance. We have access to some of their literature, in which they would report experiences of talking with Jesus in the belief that he still lived in them; they trusted these inner spiritual happenings.[2]

The Gnostics were greatly distrusted by orthodox Christians, and they were eventually discredited. The guidance of the intuitive self seemed too ephemeral, and it was felt this guidance could not be trusted. So Christian doctrine became settled around more definite beliefs about what Jesus said and did, leaving no room for new revelations from the unconscious.

I would like to propose another way of looking at this historical controversy. I want to honor the inner leadings of the Christ spirit within me. I also want to honor the time-hallowed understandings of Christian teaching. The teachings of the Gnostics were rejected because the Gnostics made the mistake of assuming that individual revelation was meant for all. If, instead, we treat our individual guidance as meaningful only for ourselves *and* test it against the traditional teachings, we may remove the objections to such insight.

If this information about the inner teacher intrigues you, perhaps you should try it in your own life. Go inside in your own meditation and see if it feels right that you should consult an inner teacher. First, lie or sit in a relaxed position. Breathe deeply, eyes closed, relaxing more with each exhalation. Then allow your awareness to follow your breath inside and down into your body. Imagine a place where you can sit on a bench by the sea or on a log in the forest. Ask your unconscious or your inner guiding figures for a teacher, and see what happens. If nothing occurs, perhaps it is not yet the time. In the workshops I offer around North America on the subject of dreams and the inner teacher, I am amazed at how many people are ready to find their inner teacher or already have some sense of it.

I suspect that the biggest danger in this whole development is that the teacher comes and is unrecognized. I often find that my friends in therapy discover their inner teacher and then the very next week forget to consult this teacher. They do not take seriously the gifts of the psyche, because we have been taught for so long to ignore them and treat them as childish nonsense. Be careful to honor the teacher within you and to learn to trust it. Turn to your teacher often, and your confidence and trust will grow.

One Teacher, or Many?

There is much discussion these days about *spirit guides*. This term was once the private property of strange, esoteric people or spiritualists. However, as we increasingly explore the unconscious through dream analysis and meditation, we find that many people are in touch with their spirit guides and are conscious of their help. And so I hear the question, "Are spirit guides the same as the inner teacher?" Or, "Is the inner teacher the same as my guardian angel?"

Who can define the landscape of the soul? I'm not sure who can answer these questions with assurance. My hunch is that spirit guides are somewhat different entities from the inner teacher, but they may function in similar ways at times. I suspect that the inner teacher is a more focused point of consciousness and wisdom than one's other guides.

And yet the inner teacher *may* be just another form of guide. As for guardian angels, I know very little.

Of one thing I am certain: If these inner figures ring true, if they work for the highest good for me and for other humans, then they are manifestations of the spirit of the living God. As for me, I insist on testing those spirits with the highest standard I know. As I am by choice a Protestant Christian, I test the spirits by the spirit of Christ as best I know it. One of another faith might use a different standard.

I believe that the task of spiritual leaders today is to instill trust of the inner teacher into our people, not to deliver the final truth. It is time for us to give up our exalted positions in order to help each person become his or her own teacher.

This book is written with the conviction that it is now the time of the inner teacher. And the teacher present in each one of us can guide us in the understanding of our dreams, as well as in the direction of our lives.

Notes
1. W. Brugh Joy, *Joy's Way* (Los Angeles: J. P. Tarcher, Inc., 1979), pp. 103-104.
2. See Elaine Pagels, *The Gnostic Gospels* (New York: Random House, 1979).

9

DREAM-SHARING GROUPS

The setting was a warm summer night, and the group members gathered in the back yard, where it seemed a little cooler. We early arrivals nibbled grapes and sipped cold drinks. When seven or eight had assembled, we sat down at a picnic table, still sharing light conversation. After we all seemed comfortable and relaxed, one member of the group, Don, asked if anyone had a dream to work on. Several people said they had a dream, and we quickly decided who should go first.

Nancy told us her dream, and several of the group made notes as she spoke. Then began a period of questions, as people in the group tried to get the details of the dream clear in their minds. After about forty-five minutes of conversation, both Nancy and the others in the group felt finished. She believed she understood the dream much better now and thanked everybody around the table.

After Nancy finished, Don told a dream he was struggling to understand, and the process was repeated until Don felt satisfied. Each dream took half an hour to forty-five minutes to process. I asked how long the group usually met. They are members of a church that sponsors three such groups. They meet every other week in someone's home, usually from 7:30 P.M. to about 9:30 P.M. They admitted that, on occasion, the closing time had ranged anywhere from 10 P.M. to 1 A.M. On occasion, the host had gone to bed and asked the group to lock the door when they left!

Several points made this group noteworthy. One was the high level of interest as the two members shared their dreams. I also noted that people shared very personal details of their lives, as well as their opinions, attitudes, and values. It was evident that they cared a lot about one another and spoke of one another fondly. Attendance in the group is fairly consistent, so members tend to know one another quite well. The dream group not only gave each individual member an opportunity to address his or her inner material, but provided a caring, supportive fellowship in which people relate quite deeply. I came away impressed with the power and potential of dream-sharing groups.

The group I had visited was one of several sponsored by Mountain View Community Church in Aurora, Colorado. In this unusual church, members struggling to know themselves are often encouraged to work with a therapist or analyst sympathetic with Jungian dream approaches. In addition, many members of the church attend one of the dream-sharing groups, which meet every two weeks. It is not uncommon to find members of this church participating in a great variety of personal growth experiences, stimulated by this basic honoring of the unconscious and the importance of each person's individuation.

Dream-sharing groups are appearing in many places now—one indication of the growing recognition of the importance of dreams and the unconscious. The Center for New Beginnings in Denver has offered classes in dream principles and dream sharing for years. At the Center for the Healing Arts in Los Angeles, dream groups have been used with cancer patients. A group of psychology professionals in Calgary, Alberta, meet every other week for an evening of dreamwork to assist members in their own personal growth.

According to Montague Ullman, "Growth centers have promoted small-group dream sharing, spontaneous and sponsored dream groups have sprung up, and a literature on the benefits and technology of dreamwork has addressed itself to the needs and interests of people who wish to work with their dreams."[1] In recent years, there have been several doctoral theses written on dream sharing, and a publication, *The Sundance Community Dream Journal,* is devoted to encouraging dreamwork, particularly in groups.[2] I have taught Jungian dreamwork principles at the Colorado Institute for Transpersonal Psychology and at the Center for New Beginnings, and have offered workshops around North America that use dream sharing in the group as a teaching method.

So the ball is rolling: Dream groups may be found in a variety of settings. Let's look more closely at this expanding phenomenon and examine some of the principles that guide dream-sharing groups.

Mountain View Groups

Mountain View Community Church (the source of the group discussed earlier) encourages the formation of its dream groups by initiating an occasional "novice" group for those who have not had experience in a dream group. A more advanced group has been meeting now for several years and is open to those who have had more exposure to dreamwork. Either the minister or an experienced leader helps the novice group get started by guiding the process in its early stages. The pastor, Dr. John Lee, has had considerable experience in dreamwork, and believes strongly in its value for personal and spiritual growth.

At a recent meeting of the advanced group, ten persons gathered in a home and sat in a circle on the floor. I asked how many usually attended the group and learned that as many as twenty-five had shown up on occasion. The usual number was eight to twelve. After some informal chatting time, the person in whose home we were meeting called the gathering to order. She began by asking who had a dream he or she wished to discuss.

Six persons raised their hands. The leader for the evening suggested that they draw from a hat to determine which ones would discuss their dreams that night. Two persons then withdrew, and it was decided that there might be time to discuss the four remaining dreams. "Who will go first?"

the hostess queried. One member volunteered to go ahead, and told us her dream.

A period of questioning, observations, suggestions, and other offerings followed. When the dreamer indicated that she had heard enough and wished to stop, the group agreed to halt. Several more times, however, someone spoke up: "I just had one more thought . . . " or "It occurred to me that. . . . " They seemed reluctant to stop, but finally did. This process was repeated with two more dreamers, and the fourth person decided not to present that evening.

Forming the background of these dream-sharing groups is a basic framework suggested in a fine article, "The Experiential Dream Group," by Montague Ullman. The author says:

> An experiential dream group is one in which people come together for the purpose of helping each other work on the feelings and metaphors conveyed by the imagery of their dreams. It is best thought of as an exercise in dream appreciation.[3]

Ullman points out that the one-to-one model of dreamwork, in which a patient consults with a psychology professional, has been the most widely used approach. The Freudian model has emphasized the need for the specialized knowledge of the professional in an attempt to avoid the dangers in dreamwork by nonprofessionals. Ullman believes there are two unfortunate results of this specialization. First, the average person has ended up with few tools to use to understand his or her dreams. Second, we have missed out on the beauty and the opportunity of sharing intimate and personal parts of our lives with a caring and interested community.

> Outside of structured therapeutic situations, there are few arrangements in life where that degree of honesty in self-disclosure can be risked in the presence of others. It is precisely this level of honesty that must be reached if one is to move beyond the constraints of one's personal emotional limitations. People in a dream

group seem to sense this, a fact that opens the way to greater and greater freedom in self-disclosure. Sharing of oneself at this level is a basic unmet need in our society.[4]

I have spoken with professionals in the psychology field who cannot imagine people sharing dreams in a group. Their experience with dream analysis in a professional therapy relationship is sometimes so intimate and deeply emotional that they cannot imagine entrusting such an important experience to the mercy of the "mob." I can only say that when one has experienced the power of a small group in which trust and caring have been established, such concerns drop away. Dream groups can be powerfully helpful, ministering agencies as truly as some professional therapists can. At the same time, a different kind of depth can emerge in a private consultation. One should not be thought of as replacing the other, since both have their place and both can serve important needs.

Ullman also states that it is the nature of dreamwork that it is best done in the presence of others. The reason, he feels, is our innate resistance to facing certain truths about ourselves. When others who care about us and who know us over a period of time point out a personality pattern or motif, it can sometimes be easier to accept.[5]

Three Basic Principles

Ullman offers three principles for experiential dream-sharing groups. The first is that the dreamer remains in charge at all times. The dreamer decides how much to reveal, what is out of bounds, and when to stop.

The second principle is that the purpose of the group is to serve the dreamer in relation to his or her own dream. This means that group members do not tell the dreamer what the dream means. They do offer their contributions but never assume authority.

The third principle stresses that the dreamer chooses to validate or not validate the offerings of group members. The dreamer has the last word about the interpretation of his or her own dream.[6]

Ullman also suggests basic guidelines for groups, and I was impressed as I saw these guidelines operating in the Mountain View group. In abbreviated form, they are:

1. Only the dreamer decides whether or not to share a dream. There is no pressure for anyone to do so.
2. Recent dreams are preferred to older dreams. With older dreams, the context is more difficult to resurrect.
3. Short dreams are better than long ones for group interaction.
4. Someone is designated to explain the process and responsibilities of the dreamer, the group, and the leader.
5. The dreamer is reminded that he or she is in charge of the situation and the interaction, and may stop when satisfied or at any other point.
6. The leader helps the group decide on which dream to discuss.
7. The group is reminded that there is a contract of confidentiality that all agree to observe. No one is to reveal anyone else's personal material outside the group.
8. The group has the opportunity to discuss general concerns, such as remembering dreams.[7]

Now let's look at the process as it might unfold in an experiential dream-sharing group using Ullman's guidelines. Let us assume a group has assembled, and the informal chit-chat period is over. The group settles down, and the leader helps the group determine who will present a dream first. Ron says he wishes to go first, and everyone agrees.

Ron tells the dream from memory, then adds details from his journal notes, using the procedure recommended by Ullman. Group members then ask Ron questions to clarify the content of the dream and to be sure they have the details accurately. The dreamer does not elaborate on his reactions at this point, but limits the presentation to the facts of the dream.

In the second stage, once the content is clear, group members begin to respond to the feelings raised by the dream and to the images found in it. Group members are reminded that they should regard their responses as their own projections, *unless* and *until* the dreamer validates those responses as his own. Ron is expected to listen receptively and to note what contributions stimulate a feeling response in him.

In the third stage, Ron tries to make the connection between his dream imagery and his life situation. He can respond to what the group has been saying and comment on his own reactions to the dream. The group then enters into conversation with Ron to explore aspects of the dream that remain unclear and to help relate it to his life. They do this with open-ended questions, and he may respond or not as he wishes. On occasion, the dreamer may be asked to recite the events of the day just before the dream. To the surprise of the dreamer, the causal factor for the dream often leaps out.

Finally, Ron evaluates what he has heard and how he now feels about the information. If he does not feel finished, the group may discuss further. Or Ron may declare that he has had enough and wishes to conclude.

Ullman's recommendation calls for groups of six to eight persons who meet weekly for two hours. He feels that a variety of persons in a group helps to enrich the process, so older and younger, male and female people should be welcome.[8]

Dream-Therapy Groups

Here is yet another model for those who wish to work more deeply with their dreams in the presence of a trained therapist. I have often led weekly dream-therapy groups, and there are some important distinctions to be made between this process and the process of a voluntary dream-sharing group. In these dream-therapy groups, I ask members to make a commitment financially and to attend weekly for a minimum of two months. This gives the group an opportunity to develop a life and style of its own. After that time, members may leave by giving the group two weeks' notice, and new members may be introduced from time to time.

I spend the initial group meeting using a variety of exercises designed to help us get to know each other and to build trust. We may also discuss the process the group will follow, what dreams have meant to us, and how best to record dreams and use a dream journal. The result is a group in which each person feels some interest and caring. We invariably do some exercises that include touching—hand contact, touching the face of a partner, giving and receiving a shoulder massage. This physical contact is very important. The result is a deepening of trust, a relaxation of competitiveness, and communication at a deeper level.

Most of us walk around in what the experts now call *beta-consciousness.* When we relax and breathe more deeply into ourselves, we drop into a deeper level of consciousness: *alpha.* In the alpha state we are more open to hear others, more able to learn, and more perceptive. It is important for the leader to be in alpha-consciousness, for it is then easier for the group to follow his or her lead. Similarly, when I meet with a person in one-to-one therapy or dreamwork, I try to be in alpha-consciousness. This helps the client to relax into that deeper state as well, and the results are much more satisfactory. Defensiveness usually drops to a minimum. If you are leading groups or doing therapy but do not know how to get yourself into alpha-consciousness, try to learn how. This one simple practice can greatly change the quality of your work.

Following the initial, get-acquainted session, the group meets for two and a half hours weekly. As in Ullman's model, I limit the group to six or eight persons. As the meeting begins, we spend about ten minutes stretching, breathing deeply, listening to our bodies, and relaxing the tensions of the day. As this warmup concludes, we join hands in a circle to connect our energies and feel the resonance among us. It is a meditative, caring connection and sets the stage for personal sharing. At times, the group has also sat quietly in meditation before beginning.

In the course of an evening, two or three persons will present a dream. The most typical pattern is for two persons to present a dream and work with it deeply; in the remaining time, several persons simply tell a dream without response.

Before we decide on dreams to present, we usually go around the circle and report on what is happening in our lives. We check in on each other and listen to shared concerns. As group leader, I report my life happenings with the others. I do not believe in leaders sitting on a pedestal, removed from life. When we have gone around the circle and listened to each other's stories, we are ready to begin. If more people wish to present than we can accommodate, we begin with the most urgent problem. We may also eliminate a person who had an opportunity to present in the previous week, in order to give the others a chance.

After the dream is presented and the group has had an opportunity to respond, I may ask the dreamer if he or she is willing to try an active imagination with one of the outstanding figures in the dream. Or I may suggest that the dreamer become one of the elements of the dream and let it speak through the dreamer's mouth. If intense emotion has come up, we may hold the dreamer in our arms while the tears flow. Great anger or rage may be worked out on a foam mattress by means of kicking and screaming to express the emotion.

In other words, we do the therapy that flows from the dream. This assumes that the dreamer is strong enough and is willing to enter into such work. I always stress that the individual is free not to enter the dream in this way. When the dreamer feels satisfied, we taper off the work and take a tea break. Individual members may now come forward to hug the tired dreamer, and we remain attuned to the feelings and emotional needs of this now-vulnerable person. We usually close the evening in a circle again, reaffirming our presence and caring to one another.

When I start a new dream-therapy group, I like to take the group away for a retreat weekend within the first two months. We usually begin on a Friday or Saturday evening, stay together in the mountains somewhere, share meals (Dot's brownies, Judine's casseroles, Charlie's homemade bread), laughter, music, and fun (even Joe's snoring), and work long and hard on dreams. This can deepen and enrich the life of the group as we become valued individuals to one another.

Dream-therapy groups such as these can be powerful experiences, if blessed with skilled leadership. I do not suggest this method for the average group of laymen wishing to know more about their dreams. The experiential dream-sharing group is a much more appropriate tool for this purpose.

One other aspect of small sharing groups: In such a group, the presence of other persons often constellates the emotional climate of one's family. Group members "become" one's brothers and sisters, mothers and fathers, aunts and uncles. This tends to raise old conflicts, old loyalties, or old memories and helps bring buried issues to the fore.

At times, in any group worth its salt, interpersonal problems will arise and need to be dealt with. In one group I led, two of the women felt an animosity that constantly intruded on the group's activity. We would occasionally need to stop the process of dream discussion and let them sit face to face in the middle of the group to work on their feelings toward each other. This process of learning can be just as valuable as the knowledge gained from dreams, and sometimes it is essential in order to move the group forward. In rare instances, such conflicts can block or freeze the group and actually prevent any therapeutic work from happening. In such cases, it is possible that the group may have to disband if the conflict cannot be resolved.

I wish to share a vision with you before closing this chapter. I imagine a wide network of dream-sharing groups for the elderly—in rest homes, churches, and senior-citizen programs. As we grow old, we often find that the things we have enjoyed over a lifetime are taken away from us—our homes, our cars, our health, our mobility, perhaps even the use of our eyes and ears. But one thing no one can ever take away from us is our dreams. To share our dreams gives us dignity and a way of being known. Our dreamwork also helps to prepare us for the experience of death, and discussing those dreams openly can lessen the fear of this transition into another form of life and help keep our minds sharp.

Dream-sharing groups for teenagers may also be an excellent way to make a connection with the thoughts, wishes, and aspirations of our youth.

People in today's impersonal, fast-paced world desperately need a place to be known by their first name, a place to be heard and honored. Dream-sharing groups, along with small groups of other kinds, could be one way to meet that great human hunger.

Notes
1. Montague Ullman, "The Experiential Dream Group," in *Handbook of Dreams: Research, Theories and Application,* ed. Benjamin J. Wolman (New York: Van Nostrand-Reinhold, 1979), p. 407.
2. Ibid.
3. Ibid., p. 406.
4. Ibid., p. 408.
5. Ibid., p. 409.
6. Ibid., p. 410.
7. Ibid., pp. 412-413.
8. Ibid., p. 421.

10

OTHER KINDS OF DREAMS

I once spoke with a young man who had had some disturbing dreams he did not understand. He was a pastor in a rural midwestern community. On a number of occasions, he had awakened in the night dreaming that a certain person in his parish had just died. To his astonishment, as he sat at breakfast the next morning, the phone would ring with the news that, indeed, such a person had died in the night. Whether this was a form of extra-sensory perception or a precognitive dream is not important. What was clear was that the information in the dream was accurate and was not available through ordinary means.

Precognitive dreams are not uncommon. I have spoken with many persons who have dreams that later come true in exact (or nearly exact) detail. How can we understand this phenomenon?

I was recently seeing a young woman in therapy who had a most unusual dream. She dreamed that she was a prisoner in a small room with an earthen floor and that a large, fat man came regularly with bits of food and used her sexually. She was a young girl of fourteen in the dream and felt hopeless about escaping. In this life, the dreamer has had difficulty relating to men. She felt, and I agreed, that this dream seemed like an episode from another life that was still affecting her present life.

Erlo van Waveren, a Jungian analyst in New York City, has published a book, *Pilgrimage to the Rebirth,* in which he discusses his past lives as they came to him through his dreams. Van Waveren discussed these dreams with Jung while doing analysis with him in Zurich many years ago. Jung encouraged him to treat them seriously.

We do sometimes find dreams in which the ordinary time dimension seems misplaced. There are dreams in which the future appears, and there are dreams that place us in ancient history. This is one of the puzzling phenomena of the unconscious—that it seems to know no time boundaries. Time appears to be a creation of consciousness, and our dream life does not seem so concerned with what time of day or time of life it is. This phenomenon can be puzzling and frightening to some.

I can share some information about precognitive dreams, though others have written of this experience in more detail. On occasion, the unconscious picks up data that the conscious mind has not recognized. I recall the man who dreamed that he saw his wife in a wedding gown, with another man as the groom. When he asked her if she were indeed planning to marry someone else, she denied it vehemently and reassured him. However, within a month or two she was involved in an affair with a man she felt she loved. She did not marry that man, but it certainly could have been her fantasy at the time of the dream. Experiences like this only underline the incredible power of the unconscious and of dreams, a power we are only beginning to accept and understand.

There are numerous recorded examples of dreams that have later come true. Jung's famous dream foreshadowing World War I is a prominent example. If you have a dream in which familiar persons are endangered, calmly tell them of your dream. Point out that it may not come true as you have dreamed it, but that you want to warn them in the event that they could take any necessary precautions. In this way, if the person ignores you and proceeds, you need not feel responsible for what happens; yet if he or she does heed the warning, you may prevent injury, harm, or even death.

There is another kind of dream I have not mentioned, but which deserves some attention. At times, a dream will come as a strong feeling without words, sounds, or images. As I slept in one of the ancient monasteries on Mt. Athos one night, I felt a strong, evil presence that came and sat on my bed. I was paralyzed by its energy and could not cry out for help. The next day, I approached this "being" in my active imagination and asked it, "Who are you, and why did you come in my dream?" It replied, "I am the spirit of all this repressed sexuality around here."

It was a memorable moment, and I will never forget it, nor how frightening it was. Yet there was no visible dream image—only a feeling. I have known others who felt a presence in the room with them in their sleep, yet did not see dream images. One woman dreamed that there was someone lying on top of her in the night, squashing the breath out of her. Her husband was asleep beside her, but she could make no sound to get his help. In her evaluation of this dream, she decided it was her shadow lying on her, trying desperately to get her attention.

On occasion, an individual will hear words from the unconscious with no visual images accompanying them. Even so, these words are treated as dreams. For example, once I was lying asleep in Zurich in a little room I had rented; it contained nothing but a tiny table, bare light bulb, and cot. That day I was to begin my Jungian analysis with Andrea Dykes, and I was very excited about it. I had set my alarm for 7 A.M., allowing myself ample time to dress, breakfast, and catch my train. However, about 6:45 I heard a voice say, "Get up!" It was so loud and clear that I opened my eyes immediately and looked around to see who was in the room. There was no one there. But I got up! My inner self was calling me to take this day seriously.

About four years ago, I heard a voice in my dream call out to me. It said, "The healing of the spirit. That is where we want you to work—the healing of the spirit." There were no images, only the voice. I knew it was an important call to the life's work which occupies my energy: to help with the healing of the spirit.

There are also waking dreams, in which we seem to be experiencing a dream-like state while fully awake. I believe this is an indication of how close we live to the unconscious. If we are relatively comfortable dealing with the unconscious and its contents, we may not make as rigid a boundary between the unconscious and our daily lives as some people do. The images may seep through during waking hours, as well as appearing in our dream time. This may also happen if the boundary between conscious and unconscious has been weakened by drug use or illness. Waking dreams can be just as valuable as sleeping dreams, and they should be recorded with the same faithfulness, if time permits. In fact, because we are awake we may capture details of the dream more clearly than when asleep.

You may want to ponder the possibility that all life is a dream, and that our dreams are reality. I urge you to consider that we may treat waking life in the same way we treat our dreams in order to understand them. You may take a life event, and look at the persons and what they represent to you, in the same way you treat a dream—using the dream journal's questions to ponder the meanings. The events of our waking lives are surely as important to analyze as our dreams are, and everyday life *is* the arena in which we live out our lives. In short, we may treat all life as a waking dream to see what we may learn from it.

An interesting example occurs in a recently published novel that portrays a mysterious, spiritual people who tell their dreams every morning and take them with utter seriousness, attempting to use the day to live out the dreams and their guidance. For them, their dream life has more reality than their waking life.[1]

Many sources also speak of *lucid dreaming*. By this they mean dreaming while asleep, but fully conscious that you are dreaming. Your conscious ego is present in the dream, aware that it is there, and able to make decisions that affect the dream situation. I have not experienced lucid dreaming and cannot comment on it with authority. Strephon Williams has a fine discussion of it in his *Jungian-Senoi Dreamwork Manual*.[2]

Many dream authorities feel that it is dangerous to attempt to make dreams turn out the way we would like them. This effort subverts the message the unconscious is trying to present to us—a message that certainly may not be pleasant to hear. The problem is that if we change the dream to come out pleasantly, we may have to face the bad news in another form. I would rather listen to my deep, wise inner self than assume that my conscious ego self knows best.

The study of dreams is a vast untapped field, ripe for harvest. We humans are a rich, deep, mysterious creation, and we know almost nothing of our potentialities as yet. Dreams are a significant avenue toward the successful exploration of the exciting inner frontier.

Notes

1. Dorothy Bryant, *The Kin of Ata Are Waiting for You* (New York: Random House, and Berkeley: Moon Books, 1971).
2. Strephon Kaplan Williams, *Jungian-Senoi Dreamwork Manual* (Berkeley: Journey Press, 1980), pp. 212-215.

DREAM-JOURNAL FORM

Created by
Clyde H. Reid,
from *Dreams:
Discovering Your
Inner Teacher*

Date of dream: _____

Title: _____ Motif: _____

The dream in detail:

(continue on back of page, if necessary)

1. Context: What is happening in my life at this time?
   _____

2. In this dream, who are the main characters known to me before?
   Name: _____
   Outstanding characteristics: _____
   What part of me is this? _____

3. Who are the main characters not known to me?
   a. Same-sex figures (= shadow?)
      _____
      _____

   b. Opposite-sex figures (anima/animus?)
      _____
      _____

4. What are the outstanding features of this dream (flood, explosion, animal, house, etc.)?

_____

_____

What part of me is this feature or image? What is it saying to me?

_____

_____

5. What important symbols appeared? How are they related to me?

_____ Notes: _____

_____ Notes: _____

_____

6. What archetypes may be manifesting themselves here?

_____

7. What feelings did I have during/after the dream?

_____

8. What other thoughts, ideas, or memories does this dream trigger in me?

_____

_____

NOTES (Summary of active imagination about this dream, or written dialogues with persons or images in the dream):

SUGGESTED READINGS

Dorothy Bryant, *The Kin of Ata Are Waiting for You*. New York: Random House, and Berkeley: Moon Books, 1971.

J. E. Cirlot, *A Dictionary of Symbols*. London: Routledge & Kegan Paul, 1962.

Marie Fay, *The Dream Guide*. Los Angeles: Center for the Healing Arts, 1978.

James A. Hall, *Clinical Uses of Dreams: Jungian Interpretations and Enactments*. New York: Grune & Stratton, Inc., 1977.

Barbara Hannah, *Encounters with the Soul: Active Imagination*. Santa Monica, Calif.: Sigo Press, 1981.

Jolande Jacobi, *Complex/Archetype/Symbol in the Psychology of C. G. Jung*. New York: The Bollingen Foundation, 1959.

W. Brugh Joy, *Joy's Way*. Los Angeles: J. P. Tarcher, Inc., 1979.

C. G. Jung, *Dreams*. Translated by R. F. C. Hull. Princeton, N.J.: Princeton University Press, 1974.

C. G. Jung, *Memories, Dreams, Reflections*. Edited by A. Jaffé. New York: Pantheon, 1963.

Emma Jung, *Animus and Anima*. New York: The Analytical Psychology Club of New York, 1957.

Maria F. Mahoney, *The Meaning in Dreams and Dreaming*. Secaucus, N.J.: The Citadel Press, 1966.

Mary Ann Mattoon, *Applied Dream Analysis: A Jungian Approach*. Washington, D.C.: V. H. Winston & Sons, 1978.

John A. Sanford, *Dreams: God's Forgotten Language*. Philadelphia: J. B. Lippincott Company, 1968.

June Singer, *Boundaries of the Soul*. New York: Doubleday and Co., Inc., 1972.

Erlo van Waveren, *Pilgrimage to the Rebirth*. New York: Samuel Weiser, Inc., 1978.

Strephon Kaplan Williams, *Jungian-Senoi Dreamwork Manual*. Berkeley: Journey Press, 1980.

Alan, Cohen   Rising in Love
Alan Cohen   The Dragon Doesn't Live Here Anymo

Scott Peck, MD.   Religion + Grace